FRANK LLOYD WRIGHT

*THE MASTERS OF
WORLD ARCHITECTURE SERIES*
UNDER THE GENERAL EDITORSHIP OF WILLIAM ALEX

ALVAR AALTO *by Frederick Gutheim*
LE CORBUSIER *by Francoise Choay*
ANTONIO GAUDÍ *by George R. Collins*
WALTER GROPIUS *by James Marston Fitch*
ERIC MENDELSOHN *by Wolf Von Eckardt*
LUDWIG MIES VAN DER ROHE *by Arthur Drexler*
PIER LUIGI NERVI *by Ada Louise Huxtable*
RICHARD NEUTRA *by Esther McCoy*
OSCAR NIEMEYER *by Stamo Papadaki*
LOUIS SULLIVAN *by Albert Bush-Brown*
FRANK LLOYD WRIGHT *by Vincent Scully, Jr.*

frank lloyd wright

by Vincent Scully, Jr.

George Braziller, Inc.   NEW YORK

Library of Congress Catalog Card Number: 60-6075

Printed in the United States of America

Ninth Printing, 1981

CONTENTS

THE AMERICAN SUBLIME

How does one stand
To behold the sublime,
To confront the mockers,
The micky mockers
And plated pairs?

When General Jackson
Posed for his statue
He knew how one feels.
Shall a man go barefoot
Blinking and blank?

But how does one feel?
One grows used to the weather,
The landscape and that;
And the sublime comes down
To the spirit itself,

The spirit and space,
The empty spirit
In vacant space.
What wine does one drink?
What bread does one eat?

—WALLACE STEVENS

FRANK LLOYD WRIGHT

IN HIS London lectures of 1939, Frank Lloyd Wright said: "Every great architect is —necessarily—a great poet. He must be a great original interpreter of his time, his day, his age."[1] Wright himself was exactly this, as he well knew when he said it. The prose of architecture—the background buildings which attempt only a little and are content to serve as neutral settings for any kind of human thought and action—did not interest him. Instead, it was his life-long intention to form human life into rhythmic patterns which seemed to him poetic and to embody those patterns in buildings which were in every case specific and unique poetic works themselves. In this double need he was the child of his time, but his extraordinary ability to carry his intentions through made him in fact its "great original interpreter."

Wright's long life's work spanned two vastly different cultural periods, and it did more than a little to bring the second of them, that of the mid-twentieth century, into being. Yet, throughout all its unique invention, it continued to recall the objectives of the first. Wright's "time, his day, his age" was that of late nineteenth-century America. He was the embodiment of its most tenacious attitudes: of its supreme confidence in the common future, and of its desperate, complementary yearning for pre-industrial, sometimes pre-civilized, images and symbols to root itself upon. This double attitude had been characteristic since the late eighteenth century of the modern world in general and of the uprooted American in particular. As such, Wright was the heir, in architecture—and regarded himself as being so—of a tradition, in part Jeffersonian, which had previously found its best expression in the works of Melville, Whitman, and Mark Twain. As they, in their writing, had celebrated at once the flux and flow which characterize modern times and the compulsion toward unity which is the democratic will, so he, in his architecture, sought to make the images of flow a fact, to celebrate continuous space, and to bring all together into shapes which were unified by his will. He himself stated the basic principle well: "Space. The continual becoming: invisible fountain from which all rhythms flow and to which they must pass. Beyond time or infinity."[2] This image of "continuous becoming," as of the river, the sea, or the prairie, was a constant in Wright's work, as it had been in that of his literary predecessors. Many streams of nineteenth-century thought, historical, biological, and philosophical, fused in it as well. To its pursuit Wright brought another nineteenth-century quality, a kind of Nietzschean individualism, not unknown in Whitman and certainly intrinsic to

Wright's friend and avowed master, Louis Sullivan. This characteristic, instinct with an arrogance Wright freely admitted, and revealing a loneliness he did his best to conceal, finds expression in one of the quotations from Whitman's *Leaves of Grass* which Wright most admired and upon which he formed his life:

Going where I list, my own master, total absolute, listening to others, considering well what they say, pausing, searching, receiving, contemplating, gently, but with undeniable will, divesting myself of the holds that would hold me. I inhale great draughts of space. The east and the west are mine, and the north and the south are mine . . . Beware of the moral ripening of nature. Beware what precedes the decay of the ruggedness of states and men. Beware of civilization.[3]

This is the mobile individual, estranged from all that is not himself, who must go forward forever, continuously forward alone, beyond both nature and civilization, which are the two major "holds" upon him. It is a most persuasive image of modern man, Auden's poets of the sea symbols, Camus' *L'Homme Révolté*.[4]

But Wright was an architect, and there were certain solid things that he loved. First, he loved the land. An examination of his work must lead us to believe that he loved it not in Whitman's way, primarily as a vast setting for the display of one's own questionable virility, but for itself, in its variety and its fact. In this love he faced a special problem, because, as Sybil Moholy-Nagy has pointed out, he was the first architect in history who was required to take on a whole continent alone.[5] Such projection of the individual into the necessity for making many and massive identifications with the world was itself appropriate and special to Wright's time. In the end he built almost everywhere on the North American continent without relinquishing his attempt to celebrate in architectural form the specific landscapes with which he happened to be involved. Characteristically, he attempted this through methods which related in principle to those which had been pursued in Bronze Age Crete, in Japan, and in Pre-Columbian America, and he admitted his admiration for the architecture of those cultures. He disliked the Hellenic way and its principles, which he refused to regard as architectural. That is, he tried, though in abstract form, to echo the shapes and dominant rhythms of the landscapes in which his buildings were set. He avoided introducing into the landscape that especially lucid image of human isolation in the world which was one of the elements of Greek architectural expression and which only a few modern architects of a later generation, most particularly Le Corbusier, have understood. The Hellenic method grew out of a complex set of religious speculations concerning the laws of nature and the life of man—a tragic perception for which Wright, along with the rest of his generation, was not prepared. It involved a recognition of separateness between things that was alien to Wright and to his time as a whole, which, as noted above, preferred to view men and nature as flowing together in a kind of evolutionary flux, like the semi-Darwinian "morphology" that Sullivan loved so well.[6]

Wright's own way was complex enough. He would at once merge with nature like a Cretan or a Japanese while, at the same time, like a Mayan, he marked off and built up abstract platforms and sculptural masses which compacted nature's shapes through human geometry and numerical control. Late in life, also, when his drive to encompass the whole of things had accelerated with the "mortal ripening" of his years, he seems to have come to understand the objectives and methods of Roman Imperial space and of the whole non-Greek Mediterranean tradition that lay behind it.

Wright's work was directly and indirectly influenced by all the architectures mentioned above, but, unlike LeCorbusier with his own influences, Wright consistently refused to acknowledge that fact. His refusal to do so was partly based upon his own tragic need, which was to keep the romantic myth of the artist as isolated creator and superman alive in himself. It also had something to do with his contempt for the generally uncomprehending and superficial use of forms from other periods (or from the magazines) which was practiced by most of the architects around him throughout his life. Yet, more deeply, his refusal to admit the help that came to him from across time grew out of his own profound loves as an architect, ideal loves which made it difficult for him to admit that he could not engross them entirely alone. Among these we have already noted his reverence for the landscape—which seemed to him to mean that each building should, ideally, be uniquely suited to its special place. We have also mentioned his desire to give precise and appropriate abstract form to the human action of his time. To these preoccupations should now be added another: his love for materials and for their expression in structures ideally appropriate to their specific natures. In this realm, which has received so much attention in the critical appreciation of Wright, he actually experienced some of his greatest difficulties, and knew that he did so.

This occurred because of a certain system of priorities—certainly not fixed, but pervasively present—which seems to have directed Wright's process of design. Looking at his developed buildings and reading his writings, we may feel that his primary interest was abstract: first, usually, in the abstraction of the space, taking shape as it did out of his double will to embody its use and to form it into a rhythmically geometric pattern. Secondly, he wished both to enclose the hollow so created and to extend it or the expression of it to the exterior through the sculptural massing of the building as a whole. Sometimes, as in the earliest works of his several phases, a concern for the exterior massing may have preceded that for the interior space. Having made his building visually integral in both its voids and its solids, he then wished to build it of such materials and in such a way as to make it structurally integral as well. In some of his later projects the structural principle may come first in the process, but when we survey his work in general we find that structural integration tended to come last at any stage in his development and that he himself was most specifically pleased with any building when its structural rather than simply its spatial and sculptural aspects were intrinsic to the whole. This helps explain Wright's admiration for buildings such as the early "Romeo and Juliet" windmill and the Imperial Hotel, which otherwise seem either of small importance or of doubtful success. Conversely, he was always willing to force or conceal the structure when he had to in order to achieve his spatial and sculptural ends. Yet he never relinquished his ideal of integration, and his pleasure at his successes is indicative of his deepest intent. He clearly believed that, when a building built by men to serve a specifically human purpose not only celebrated that purpose in its visible forms but became an integrated structure as well, it then took on the character of an organism which existed according to its own complete and balanced laws. In this way it dignified by its wholeness and integrity the purely human intellect and hand which had created it. This is what Wright meant by "organic." Few architects have attempted so much and have been willing to ignore so little in order to achieve it.

The principles governing Wright's design which have been noted above can best be clarified and expanded through a roughly chronological consideration of some of his buildings. The principle of abstraction came to him early. In 1876, at the Philadelphia Centennial Exposition of that year, his mother discovered the Froebel Kindergarten method, with its system of building blocks, folded paper, strings, and beads.[7] Wright, then seven years of age, worked and played with these objects throughout the rest of his childhood. Manson has pointed out how closely the constructed forms to which the Froebel materials lent themselves were echoed by many of Wright's mature designs[8] (plate 1). At the Centennial, too, were reproductions of American Colonial houses, some English Queen Anne work, and a Japanese pavilion. Influences from all these sources were to play a part in the development of the domestic Shingle Style of the eighteen-eighties, out of which Wright's earliest work directly grew.[9] We must assume, however, that he was looking at buildings from his earliest childhood. His mother would certainly have encouraged this. Indeed, she had determined pre-natally that her son should be an architect and had, to that end, hung engravings of the great cathedrals in her room. Later they were transferred to Wright's room. This triumph of nineteenth-century applied psychology, in which the son became the builder—as well as the contempt for his father which was also instilled in him—must have had much to do with creating both Wright's self-confidence and his isolation.

In 1876, the kind of domestic design the young Wright might have seen is typified by the houses that were published in the Pattern Books of the period (plate 2). These also owed a good deal to Gothic Revival theory, as interpreted mechanistically by Viollet-le-Duc and others. Thus, when built in wood, they tended to concentrate upon an expression of their structural skeleton, creating that characteristic web of thin members which I have elsewhere named the "Stick Style."[10] Totally articulated, light and impermanent like so much American building of all periods, these houses formed the vernacular base against which the consciously professional architects of the Shingle Style reacted. A desire for both continuity and permanence and, eventually, for strong, closed, abstract order, was implicit in that reaction. The forms of Richardson, whether built of rough stone or of wood frame sheathed with shingles, show those several characteristics (plate 3). The separate shapes—horizontal window bands, triangular gables, and cylindrical towers—are compacted into one powerful mass, expressed as a continuous heavy shell around a deep volume of space and penetrated by a cavernous archway. Such buildings seemed to assert that Americans had been upon their continent forever, belonged there, and were what they in fact had never been, deeply rooted in the land. By 1885, many architectural publications were reproducing photographs of shingled houses where such compact abstraction and expression of permanence were clear to see (plates 4, 5). Wright, after having read, he tells us, Ruskin, Viollet-le-Duc, and Owen Jones,[11] and having spent something under two years in engineering school at Madison, Wisconsin, went to Chicago and worked for James Lyman Silsbee, an architect of the Shingle Style. He soon left Silsbee and entered the office of Adler and Sullivan, but when, in 1889, he built his own house in Oak Park, he modelled it closely upon the published designs of two shingled houses of 1885–86 by Bruce Price, at Tuxedo Park, New York (plates 6, 7). The two bays of Wright's facade derived from Price's Chandler House, as I have shown elsewhere,[12] but his general proportions are closer to those of Price's Kent House, which is reproduced here (plates 4, 5). We should note that it was the abstract clarity of Price's exterior to which Wright was sensitive at this time. He was not yet interested in the abstract spatial order, created by cross-axes, which existed in Price's plan. Wright's own interior was therefore considerably less coherent than Price's and broke less out of "the box" than Price's had already done. But it does show, in its handling of partitions as separated panels under a continuous horizontal molding (derived during the seventies and eighties from the Japanese *kamoi* and *ramma*) a clear understanding of how to open up but still articulate interior space as that technique had been developed and published by Stanford White and other architects during the eighties.[13] The twin themes of spatial continuity and geometric order are thus both explicitly stated but totally unintegrated in Wright's first significant personal design.

The general movement toward order which took place during the eighties led many architects toward the Renaissance for inspiration. It is well known how this movement culminated in the Beaux-Arts eclecticism of the Chicago World's Fair of 1893 and of most later monumental and even domestic building of the early twentieth century. For a brief period, however, sympathy for the Renaissance produced highly original work, where the principle of order and clarity was seen in essential rather than representational terms.[14] A house in New York, by McKim, Mead and White, of 1887, is indicative of this (plate 8). Sullivan's own Wainwright Building of 1890–91 is not far different in many ways (plate 9). The cleanly pierced stone sheathing of the first floors, the fine, thin Roman brick of the intermediate walls or piers, the panelled ornament, the projecting cornice, even the handling of the windows of the central portion as grouped in a plaited panel, are all common to both buildings. Sullivan's achievement was, of course, far greater, because he was extending order into new programs and was making apparent the splendid structural and spatial body which the skyscraper office building could be. Clearly enough, Wright's Charnley House, done by him for his firm in 1891, owes something to both these buildings (plate 10). Again, the stone sheathing of the base changes to Roman brick which is capped by a clean cornice. The windows are sharp-edged throughout, but now they seem cut into a solid. There is no plaiting, no panelling. Contrasted with Sullivan's blooming web in cladded steel and with McKim, Mead and White's razor thin facade, Wright's building is a dense compacting of blocks. Once again the Froebel training seems apparent (plate 1). In a sense, Wright, at twenty-two, was already more abstract than his predecessors.[15]

The next problem to be conquered was that of spatial continuity, its extension to the exterior, and the expression of it in the building as a whole. The Winslow House, of 1893, Wright's first commission on his own after he left Adler and Sullivan (his first of many divestings of "the holds that would hold" him) shows experiments in those directions (plates 11–13). Its basic plan and massing are symmetrical, and the street facade is a beautiful demonstration of the pure placing of openings in a wall. The house opens outward toward the rear in plan and massing, however, and the void of a porch is incorporated into its plan, though not into its volume, as many earlier architects of the Shingle Style had done. A geometrical play of opposing shapes is also set up in this area, with the great overhang of the roof intersecting the vertical polygon of the stair tower. Wright was beginning to interweave his elements, indicating a flow of volumes from one to the other. The band of ornament on the second floor also assists the cornice in denying the boundaries of the walls. That is, its broken surface texture splinters the light and sets up a play of shadows which denies any sense of structural solidity to the wall under the overhang. This then, itself assisting that effect by the shadow it casts over the visually non-structural zone, seems partly to float above the solid base of the ground floor. Sullivan was sometimes to use his ornament for similar effects, as in the Carson-Pirie-Scott Store of 1899–1904, where he visually separated the upper floors from the ground below by such ornamental masking of the structural solidity of that zone. In the Winslow House Wright was attempting, by ornament and at a very early date, to achieve that expression of spatial continuity and that "destruction of the box" which he was later to achieve in more integral ways.

The Husser House, of 1899, represents a further step, again in masonry (plates 14, 15). The plan, more geometrically powerful than that of the Winslow House, now also resembles advanced types published during the eighties, especially some by Wilson Eyre, of Philadelphia.[16] It is extended in a long horizontal axis and continued by a porch. A weaker, off-set, cross axis houses the stair tower and dining room bay and is expressed upon the exterior, so that the building is no longer a contained block but an intersection of thin, outward-reaching masses. Ornament still floats the widely overhung roof above the heavily silled lower floors, but Wright now opens the projected corners with window bands. Then, as if dismayed by his temerity, he encases those voids in a grotesquely scaled arcade. The projected porch of the second floor has a difficult intersection with the wall behind it and suggests the structural as well as plastic problems which were not yet integrated in the design.

By about 1900 Wright had solved the complex and—by then it had become apparent —revolutionary problem he had posed himself. The fact that he solved it first in houses of wood frame construction may be significant. It will be recalled that his beloved windmill for the family's farm at Spring Green had been built in 1896 (plate 16). Its primary characteristic is a union of structure with powerfully abstract form. A vertical pole is anchored deep in the rock and stabilized laterally by a lozenge-shaped casing. A polygonal, hollow shell, containing a stair, then embraces the lozenge and completes the lateral wind-bracing of the whole. Wright's reason for naming this double structure "Romeo and Juliet" is perhaps franker than might have been expected for the period but need puzzle no one, as, inexplicably, it seems to have done.[17] In 1898 Wright built the River Forest Golf Club and enlarged it in 1901 (plates 17, 18). As completed, it has a clear, cross-axial plan, somewhat reminiscent of Price's for the Kent House (plate 5). The spatial axes are continued by terraces and defined by low, overhanging hip roofs which are supported only by the wooden posts of the structural frame. Windows are then set between each post, so that a continuous horizontal void now appears in fact below the continuous plane overhead. The planes of wall also express spatial continuity by their horizontal board and batten sheathing. The building is very low, so that it not only enhances the ground plane but also forces the eye of the observer outside or in to follow its horizontal extensions. In this way the scale is forced down and the continuous rather than the volumetric quality of the space is stressed—except in the octagonal lounge, which was added in the second project as a higher, climactic spatial volume.

The American tradition of wood frame structure then played its part in the first great masterpiece among the Prairie Houses. This was the Ward Willitts House, of 1902, which may, if it was in fact designed earlier than the Hickox and Bradley Houses at Kankakee, be the earliest of the Prairie Houses as well (plates 19, 20, 54). Its exterior is articulated by, and its windows set within, an expression of its wooden skeleton, and it seems to recall in this way the Stick Style tradition of Wright's childhood (plate 2). At the same time, its use of light-colored stucco panels between darker stripping seems to mirror Japanese forms as well. Wright has always insisted that he was influenced only by Japanese prints, but, as many writers have pointed out, the Ho-o-den at the Chicago Fair of 1893 seems a likely candidate for a share in the ancestorship of the Willitts House[18] (plate 21). This seems true in plan as well. The interlocked cross axes of the Japanese building recur almost exactly in Wright's design. At the same time the latter also seems to pick up what Price's plan had to offer, a perception for which Wright had not been prepared in 1889 (plate 5). But the Wright plan differs from the other two in its abstract decision and its confident, even compulsive, sweep. As in the Golf Club, a fireplace mass now occupies the center. It is the solid shaft, celebrated by Melville, which rises through the hollow of the house.[19] Such placing of the massive chimney was common in American Colonial practice. Its use by Wright may partly derive from the same sources which had inspired the Colonial Revival from 1876 onward. It, too, sought rootedness and permanence. Wright himself said: "It comforted me to see the fire burning deep in the solid masonry of the house itself. A feeling that came to stay."[20] The spaces of the Willitts House extend out from the fire in directed channels and are continued by terraces and porches. That continuity of axis is then fully enforced by the horizontal planes of the interior and exterior alike. The interior trim, interweaving around the central core, completely carries out the spatial motif and, in a curious way, turns space and building fabric into one interwoven whole (plate 28).

The importance of the Willitts House as an image of modern times can best be shown by contrasting it with a sixteenth-century central plan where cross axes were used (plate 22). In Palladio's Villa Rotunda the center of the house is a cylindrical void, rather than Wright's massive solid. Thus, in the Palladian design, the human being can occupy the center of the house; in Wright's, he is in flow around an already occupied center. From the Palladian central space doors upon all four sides allow long axial vistas for the view. But there can be little sense of compulsion to move toward those views, because the central void rises high above the side openings and creates a stable, vertical volume of space which dramatizes the upright human being at its center and keeps him fixed where he is. Finally, the exterior cube contains the whole. In Wright's house the occupant's eye is compelled to move out on the horizontal, and he himself is in a space which is only just high enough to allow him to stand upright in it, so that he will eagerly seek out the long, serene horizontals which offer the euphoria of his only spatial release. The light, too, gently draws his attention as he sits near the fireplace, in a dimness like that of the early colonial houses, and it is led outward toward the comparative, but still muted, brightness of the tinted window bands and the voids of the porches.

The Palladian plan is an excellent expression of a pre-industrial, humanistic world where the human being occupied a fixed, central position. The Wright plan is an image of modern man, caught up in constant change and flow, holding on, if he feels he must, to whatever seems solid, but no longer regarding himself as the center of the world. Wright's is most of all a specifically American image. The axes are like country cross roads in the boundless prairie, or like Bingham's long rafts sliding down out of the picture under the continuous sky on the stream of the river, or like Huck and Jim on the Mississippi, where they find comfort only while floating onward together through the mists and where all turns to nightmare whenever they touch the shore.[21]

So, at the corners of the Willitts House, the posts, otherwise abstractly expressed in the stripping, are withdrawn, and the windows themselves are set back in plane, so that the walls tend to become merely space-defining screens and the roofs go outward continuously: "floating," and expressing that continuity of space around which the whole building was now integrated. Wright himself later stated his intentions here, and he aimed his attack precisely against the classic idea of the columned pavilion with defined corners. "Have no posts, no columns," he wrote. Or again: "In my work the idea of plasticity may now be seen as the element of continuity." And again, "Classic architecture was all fixation ... now ... let walls, ceiling, floors become seen as component parts of each other, their surfaces flowing into each other." He continued, "Here ... principle entered into building as the new esthetic, continuity," and he hailed "... the new reality that is *space* instead of matter."[22] This new space he called "The Architecture of Democracy," and in exactly that sense its overall continuities, compulsive and mesmeric upon the individual, would have been understood, I think, by De Tocqueville and Whitman alike.

In the Willitts House, therefore, Wright had absorbed his tradition and the earlier influences upon him. He had arrived at the first maturity of his intentions and his means and had become "a great original interpreter of his time." The house and its plan, with many flexible variations, served as a kind of type model for numerous later Prairie Houses, as the first Jacobs House was to do for the "Usonian" houses of Wright's later years. But Wright could never rest upon types. In 1902, for example, in the Heurtley House (as in the Hillside Home School at Spring Green, of the same year), he solved his masonry problem (plate 23). Here the dense, closed mass which Richardson had used (plate 3), but which was now unsympathetic to Wright in terms of the spatial continuity he desired, was broken up into vertically standing but horizontally stripped planes, clearly differentiated one from the other and with long horizontals spanning between them or supported by them. The fabric now becomes spatially and structurally interwoven under the low-hipped frame roof which caps it. As much as any building by Richardson, the Heurtley House is an earth-pressing mass and a dark cave, with a deep, low entrance whose arch is echoed by that of the central fireplace within (plate 24). The interior space is a cave above which the taut, wood-stripped ceiling stretches its opposite, a tent.

During the same year, the roof as volume-defining hip disappeared entirely in the Yahara Boat Club Project, also designed for masonry construction (plate 25). The lower walls advance upon their broad platform, and those supporting the long, flat roof stand behind and rise above them, so that the extended horizontal of the roof plane not only unifies the solids and voids below it but also seems to float free above the plane of the platform itself. In the Martin House, at Buffalo, of 1904, the masonry planes were turned into free-standing piers (plates 26–28). Smaller verticals rise between them and help support horizontal brick panels which are, visually, woven into them. The widely over-hung, low-hipped roofs conceal steel beams within them, but they so obviously complement in space the vertical shafts of the piers that the eye can accept them as intrinsic abstract components and the mind does not worry too much about their actual construction. The great piers integrally form the spaces of the house and march outward to group again in far-flung subsidiary colonies (plate 27). They now structurally articulate the main cross axis of the living areas by gathering into groups of four at its intersections (plate 28). In this way they also integrally form what Louis I. Kahn was later to call "service spaces" between them, since radiant heating panels are set in the small squares they define.[23]

Vertical brick piers and wall planes also made possible the splendid integration of space, structure, and massing which Wright achieved in the Larkin Company Office Building at Buffalo, of 1904 (plates 29–32). In space the building was conceived of as facing inward, with a glass-roofed central hall rising the entire height and with horizontal office floors woven around it. The pattern of piers and walls which makes these spaces is clearly unified in both plan and section. The vertical piers rise uninterruptedly inside, and the horizontal planes of the office floors are kept back from their edges, so that they seem, once more, to be woven through them. Stairways are grouped in vertical shells of wall at the four corners of the building, which then reveals all these articulations upon its exterior: the big piers, the smaller ones between them, the horizontal spandrels and the corner towers, expressed purely as free-standing space containers at the edges of the main, interwoven mass. Contrast should be made with Sullivan's somewhat similar Wainwright Building (plate 9) where it was the expression of the fabric as a muscular, skeletal body with a beginning and an end which was being attempted. In the Larkin Building it was the fabric as container and definer of space that was stressed. The Wainwright Building thus has a kind of humane glow; the Larkin Building was a hollowed, galleried cliff. This is one reason why it could have no high base and no cornice, although Wright brought it grandly to a halt by his indication of an attic.

Entrance was at the side, under a portal set back between the main mass and the thin, subsidiary office block, from the end of which a metallic sheet of water sprang. Here Wright achieved one of the first of his monumental spatial sequences. The exterior is challenging and rather forbidding, but it tells us that something is contained inside. Entrance to it must be sought. It is finally found in the dark place behind the fountain. The block is thus penetrated surreptitiously as it were, and essentially from below. The advance is from outer light toward interior dimness beyond which, to the left, somewhat more light could be perceived filtering down between the central piers. These then rise up toward their rich capitals in a climactic spatial expansion, lighted from above as in Roman buildings and creating, as those also did, an idealized interior space cut off from the world outside. At the same time, the stiff verticals of the interior of the Larkin Building continued to recall the challenge of the exterior, so that the occupant could not feel himself to be simply inside a shell. The sequence was an emotional one and a progress: challenge, bafflement, compression, search, and finally, surprise, release, transformation, and recall. It was almost a Baroque progression, but its methods were stiffer and harder, befitting the industrial program which they praised. Significantly enough, the building also recalled the Romantic-Classic projects of the first revolutionary architects of the later eighteenth century, particularly in the harshness of its forms but even in the rather underscaled world globes which were flaunted upon its exterior.[24]

Unity Church, of 1906, also creates an ideal interior space, and it does so, like the Larkin Building, through an organization of wall planes and piers (plates 33–35). As an abstract mass it is much denser than the other. Its exterior both closes and opens, protecting but expressing the rich interweaving of spaces inside. It is not challenging but at once secret and full of promise. Though uncompromisingly monumental it is scaled to the individual rather than to the office hive. The concrete of the exterior has a pebbled aggregate which makes it sympathetic to the touch. The building thus encloses and invites. Its union of these opposites must have seemed to the free-thinking congregation for which it was built an ideal expression of the character of modern religious experience. In his *Autobiography* Wright has described with admirable lucidity how he assembled the poured concrete elements of the structure in order to form the space he desired.[25] That space is again a hieratic progress: along a slightly raised platform at the side between two blocks, under a low entrance, into a dark place beyond which, after a tortuous passage, the main meeting place opens as an embracing room. Four piers stand at the corners within the shells of outer wall, and balconies are woven between them. These are low, as in Colonial meeting houses, and here, as there, the congregation is brought close to the preacher in its tightly packed square. The interweaving of main masses and details now becomes symphonic, itself a hymn full of deep chords and complicated polyphonic passages. But the general effect is calm. The light is almost golden from the tinted skylights above, warmly alive with Froebel patterns and integrally set between the crossed concrete beams of the ceiling structure. In Unity Temple, therefore, Wright was interpreting both his time and its memories. In terms of the history of Protestantism on this continent it still remains the most modern and the most traditional church built in twentieth-century America. It is a mighty fortress at individual scale, for the individual who, however packed in with others, remains spiritually alone.

It is impossible to discuss the many other successes of Wright's Oak Park years. His design became richer and clearer. The delicate proportions of the Hardy House, with its three levels poised on the side of a hill above Lake Mendota, and rendered by Wright as an incident in a Japanese screen; the elaborate but serene interweaving of lower and higher spaces and masses in the Coonley House (plate 36); the interlocked two stories of space in the Roberts House (plate 37); the clean advance and recession of light-colored planes in the Gale House (plate 38) are all examples of the harvest of this first maturity. By 1908–1909 Wright made his strongest statement in domestic design. The Robie House lifts its dark and compulsively extended living room floor in one long axis but pins it firmly to the earth through the shorter cross axis of its fireplace mass (plates 39–41). The central solid and its long tradition seem now to be holding the rest of the building down, as it seeks, like an airplane, to take wing. The two persistent American images, the first of mobility—of flight, of "getting away"—the second of rootedness and security, are now locked together in one climactic work that culminates a century or more of American art. At the same time the brick masses of the lower floor, solid and heavy, are being lifted too on their steel beams, like those which support the wide cantilevers above. Entrance is at the rear, so that the whole composition toward the street can remain one of pure and unbroken horizontals rising in tiers. The meaning embodied by them would seem again to be double: it is first of the earth, with its clefts, hollows and climactic masses, felt as full of life, always moving and lifting itself like some great beast, as Cézanne saw it (plate 42). The second meaning grows out of the first. As the earth and objects upon the earth are pulled into the rhythm of flux and change, it and they fragment into their components, which then oscillate around each other in an "eternal becoming." This is the world as the cubists saw it (plate 43). The Robie House thus combines Cézanne's reverence for the majesty of solid things and his recognition of the forces that pull at them with Picasso's and Braque's fragmentation of solids into planes which move continuously through space. Lacking contact with these contemporary European expressions in painting, Wright was still creating many of the same meanings with his forms.[27]

Appropriately, the Robie House marks a kind of terminal point for the first phase of Wright's career. Up until 1909 he had been part of a tradition, which he brought to fruition but in whose cultural ambiance he was imbedded all the same. In 1909 the counter urge toward "getting away" became too strong, and he divested himself once more of the holds upon him, left his large family and went to Europe with another lady. Impelled to do this, he still felt, in a very American way, the necessity to justify himself before public opinion at large.[28] Upon his return, in 1911, he built a large house for his new family upon his mother's family's land at Spring Green, Wisconsin. Taliesin, (or Taliesin North, as he later came to call it) seems very much a place of return and a waiting place (plates 44–46). Its long, quietly hipped roofs, sliding over horizontal window bands and flatly laid stone piers, embrace the brow of a considerable but gentle hill above a river and with a broad but undemanding view across the valley on the other side. The forms of the building, throughout all its later transformations, remained much less abstract than many of Wright's earlier works had been. They were gentle too, and defined a courtyard space, partly cut off from the view by house and hill top, where the occupant could feel protected and withdrawn. The living room was part cave and part pavilion. Taliesin was thus the expression of a return, beyond the suburb, not only to the land of the only ancestors Wright would acknowledge and to a house named "Shining Brow" in their tongue, but also to his beloved Jeffersonian tradition of the moral strength to be derived from the earth. In its own way, Taliesin was the successor of Monticello.

But Wright could not live by cultivating his acres, and the continuation of his life's work forced him, ironically, almost into a commuter's pattern. The forms of the buildings he did in Chicago at this time are often the opposite of those at Taliesin. They are generally more, not less, abstracted than the earlier works. The Coonley Playhouse of 1912 is an excellent example among several (plates 47, 48). The plan is more purely like that of the Ho-o-den than any of the earlier cross-axes had been (plate 21). Its symmetry is a recurrent theme during these years. Upon the exterior the dark-stained wooden cantilevers penetrate the main volumes of the building and extend outward from them with an almost impatient decision. Such command approached *hybris* in the grandiloquent Midway Gardens Restaurant of 1914 (plates 49, 50). Here the horizontal brick masses of the Robie House were relieved of their hipped roofs and were widely stretched between massive towers. Above these, complicated stick work interlocked, and thin flagstaffs, like the barge and fishing poles of nineteenth-century American painting, rose as thin verticals against the empty sky. Pavilions sat at the corners, and the whole fabric enclosed a vast terrace, to be used for outdoor dining, band concerts, and so on. Abstracted, though rather sentimental, sculptured figures looked down on the scene. The setting for outdoor city-living which Midway Gardens created was thus pervaded by all the most typically American imagery we have already discussed. Its destruction after Prohibition killed its function and marked in its own way the end of an expansive era.

The tragedy which occurred at Taliesin in 1914, more terrible than that which struck Oedipus, has been described by Wright (*An Autobiography,* pp. 184–86) in some of the most restrained and moving writing ever done in America—and was democratically recognized by various persons of the region as the inevitable punishment for differentness and sin. It made it essential for Wright, as he tells us, to withdraw further from his earlier life than had been necessary before. The refuge upon the Jeffersonian farm had proved illusory, and he was now forced to take the typical modern journey, as a lonely man travelling physically in space and psychically in time. The providential offer of the commission for the Imperial Hotel in Tokyo took him in 1915 to Japan, where he spent much of the next five years. The Imperial Hotel embodies to the full Wright's concept of interlocked and flexible cantilever construction (plates 51–53). As noted earlier, he was always pleased with it, and, to his joy, it rode out the great earthquake of 1922. Its interwoven spaces recall those of Midway Gardens, but its details, carved in a soft lava stone, are much richer and more complicated, probably too rich and over-scaled. Like those of the Midway Gardens, they may seem more Mayan than Japanese —mirroring an influence upon Wright which we shall discuss later. The scale of the whole Imperial Hotel complex is rather oppressive, weighing down, extending, inter-weaving, and proliferating as it does. In it Wright seems to have arrived at a moment when, for the first time in his life, he could only elaborate upon what he had done before.

While this was happening to him in the 'teens the influence of his earlier work was spreading in Europe. The Wasmuth publications of 1910 and 1911 precipitated that development.[29] In 1914 Gropius had already built an adaptation of the Mason City Bank and the Yahara Boat Club project in his model factory at the Werkbund Exhi-bition in Cologne. Both the Wright buildings had been published by Wasmuth[30] (plate 25). Dutch architects, too, were producing a good deal of work closely based upon Wright's designs. In my opinion the Dutch De Stijl movement itself owed even more to Wright's interwoven stripping details and plastic masses (plate 38) than it did to French cubism. The rhythmic patterns of sliding lines and planes which Van Doesburg developed may be closest of all to Wright at this period, but it was Mondrian who cul-minated the process. Even his mature work of the early twenties forms patterns which are not so different from those created by Wright many years before (plates 54, 55). Like Wright, Mondrian claimed that he was seeking an abstract formulation which could image both the continuity implicit in and the stability to be wrested from, mod-ern times.[31] His long, crossing lines, his tensely balanced proportions, and his planes of primary color, were all expressive of an order larger than themselves, and they became the inspiration for much of the planning, massing, and surface treatment of the "Inter-national Style" architecture of the twenties and thirties. One European architect at least was capable of learning spatial lessons from Wright. Mies Van der Rohe's projected house plan of 1923 (plate 56) adopts the Wrightian cross axis (plate 20), extends it con-tinuously outward, but interrupts it rhythmically and spaces its solid components in ways which seem to derive from De Stijl experiments of the teens. At the same time it should be noted that Mies' definition of space by asymmetrically separated wall planes, while differing from most of Wright's previous work, can be matched by a few of his early plans, as by that for the Gerts House of 1906 (plate 57). Mies' Barcelona Pavilion of 1929, in which the old Yahara Boat Club project took on new spatial and structural form, was a more developed synthesis of American influence and European sensibility. Its flowing space, wholly asymmetrical but clearly deriving from the "Open Road" con-tinuity of Wright, was now effectively contained by closed end walls, like those of a European garden (plate 58). The American desire for movement, and the European instinct for permanence, found their modern "International" union here.

Elsewhere I have attempted to describe Wright's influence and its transmutation by the Europeans in more detail.[32] We shall return to that relationship again, but it should only be noted that Wright's disapproval of the new European design was based upon more than personal pique. Its clarified, simplified forms necessarily appeared to him to be "almost nothing." He thought also, following lines we have ourselves sketched above, that he had already done it all himself anyway and so what was the fuss all about. He was wrong; he had not done what the younger architects were doing. They were Europeans and men of a later generation. Their view of the world was intellectualized, ironic, and self-criticizing in a way that Wright could never have understood. Their forms showed this, as much in what they avoided as in what they did. They announced a new age and its new attitude, through which men faced the harshness of twentieth-century reality in terms of conscious exposure to it. In accordance with this, some of them romanticized the machine and cut themselves off from older ties with a puritan strictness Wright had never exercised. A few, especially the Bauhaus group but certainly not Le Corbusier, seemed for a time even to fear nature and memory as they isolated themselves and their forms from both. All this was foreign to Wright's late nineteenth-century belief in flowing oneness and serenity and inimical to the whole titanic struggle to make things one in which he remained engaged.

His struggle during the teens and twenties was especially severe. He had lost or outgrown his tradition and his place. The American culture which had quite freely supported experiment up to the time of the First World War was beginning to become more timid. The suburb lost to him, he now needed new roots to fix himself upon the continent. In a book begun in 1915, finished in 1922, D. H. Lawrence was to write that the true "Spirit of the Place" in America was held by the surviving Indians and that, with their passage, it would enter overtly into the soul of the white man and "the full force of the demon of the continent" would be released.[33] By 1915, at least, Wright had already attempted to tap that force, and was openly seeking inspiration from Indian forms. Tselos, who, among others, has pointed this out, feels that influences from pre-Columbian architecture can be detected in Wright's work of a much earlier period.[34] This may be true, but the first clearly overt use of such forms occurred in the A. D. German Warehouse of 1915 (plate 59). Here the solid brick block is pierced by three narrow slits, above which a cast concrete mosaic models a rich attic with a pronounced outward batter. All these details are directly matched in such a Mayan building as the "Temple of the Two Lintels," at Chichen Itza, in Yucatan[35] (plate 60). The direct borrowing is obvious. What Wright wanted is also clear: maximum mass, sculptural weight, a monumentality even more dense and earth-pressing than he had achieved before—and one more primitive, separate from his earlier culture, exotic to his eyes, and deep in time. It was a monumentality, moreover, which held in it no reference, however abstracted, to the human body, as the Doric column did. Its references, beyond those to the monumentalized hut, were to the compacted hill, thus to non-human nature, not to man (plate 62). Its use allowed Wright to remain outside the tradition of humanist design and to continue to evoke by his forms the natural settings in which men move rather than the human body itself. This was again anti-Hellenic, and our earlier contrast between the Wainwright and Larkin buildings should return to mind (plates 9, 29, 30).

The program of the A. D. German Warehouse could encourage the maximum mass with minimal opening which most Mayan architecture exhibited. What of the house, the human ambient itself? The Barnsdall House, in Hollywood, designed while Wright was in Japan and built in 1920, attempted to answer that question, as did several other projects at that time (plate 61). The Barnsdall House invokes Mayan temples as published in archaeological drawings or as they could have been seen in plaster models as early as the Chicago World's Fair of 1893 (plate 62). Its platform is compressed, and the Mayan geometricized hill mass, a near-solid of concrete, is made hollow through the imitation of it in stuccoed wood frame construction. In a sense Wright was starting all over again here with the desired abstract massing and the closed volume of space, almost as he had begun, though with much less forcing, in the Charnley House of 1891 (plate 10). But Wright would not leave it at that. By 1923 he had found an integral structural system through which to create the enclosing volume and to give it Mayan monumentality and richness of surface mosaic (plate 60). His Millard House, in Pasadena (plates 63, 64), was the first to use his invention of hollow, pre-cast concrete blocks, plain, patterned, or perforated, which were strung through with steel rods and then filled, where desired, with poured concrete. In this system the concrete forms and the wall surface were one, and the final fabric, with its rods, could take both compression and tension and might therefore be used for walls and spanning members alike. It also produced an integral surface which did not suffer with the staining and weathering of time. Strikingly enough, the Millard House, with its closed wall planes and its two-storied living area—opening like the megaron of a Mycenaean lord only in one direction—resembles Le Corbusier's Citrohan projects of the year before (plate 65). Le Corbusier's first use of the supporting columns, as well as his projecting terrace, are also recalled in the much more plastic and integrated piers and balcony of the Wright design. A roof terrace, Mediterranean or Californian, is common to both. Wright in 1923, therefore, whether through knowledge or accident, was coming close to the early experiments of the architect who in general embodied principles most counter to his own and who was to become his most important twentieth-century rival.

Wright went on to exploit his block system in many other houses which were as appropriate as the Millard House to the California landscape. In the Storer House he developed the blocks as piers and opened the building into an articulated pavilion; in the Freeman House he dramatized the system with great beams and elaborated the patterns and perforations of surface which the blocks made possible (plate 66). The Ennis House used its hill as a Mayan temple base and loomed at the top like something from Tikal. But the twenties were not rich in commissions for Wright, and his sometimes rather desperate search for stimulus led him to other Indian forms, as in the Lake Tahoe Summer Colony project of 1922, where the cottages not only closely evoked the shapes of the pines around them but also resembled the tepees of the Plains Indians (plate 67). Their conical tents also inspired the shapes of the Nakoma Country Club project, of 1924. Indian inspiration and a sense for the tree as a construction rather than simply as a shape, would together seem to have brought Wright to one of his greatest projects: the St. Mark's Tower of 1929 (plates 68, 69). This apartment building recalled and perfected the old "Romeo and Juliet" windmill, sank its concrete root deeply into the earth, and rose from it as a hollow trunk with four projecting fins of wall. Interlocked, two-story apartment floors were cantilevered out from the vertical bearing elements, and the spaces so created were to have been sheathed in glass and copper, above which the wall fins rose like Mayan roof combs. St. Mark's Tower, rising like a jewel out of some of Wright's most tormented years, best expresses of all his projects the structural, spatial, and formal abstraction through which he hoped to evoke nature's organic forms. His own words describe it, "... Dignified as a tree in the midst of nature, but a child of the spirit of man."[36] The depression of 1929 killed it, but a later version—its prismatic elegance severely injured by a complication of its function, by vertical and horizontal sun screens, and by gross detailing in general—was finally built in 1953 as the Price Tower at Bartlesville, Oklahoma.

His culture having fallen away from beneath him once more, this time in a financial collapse which eliminated the clients he had begun again to assemble, Wright set himself during the idle years to the creation of an ideal culture and its architectural setting. His Broadacre City, (plate 70) first exhibited in 1935, spread the suburb out across the countryside, rationalized it somewhat with a mixture of manufacturing units and Jeffersonian farms, and sprinkled it with small houses on acre plots and with St. Mark's Towers for those inhabitants who might as yet be inadequately agrarianized. Large houses were to sit, in the old tradition, upon the highest ground, and a project for one of these, the "House on the Mesa," in its cubical planarities and spread out separation of units both in plan (plate 71) and massing, now seems to show influence upon Wright from the European architects whom he himself had influenced earlier.[37] Wright has never admitted such receptivity, quite the contrary, but it would seem to have existed in fact, and its effect was to help him—as he had helped the Europeans earlier—to clarify and redirect his design. The thirties became one of his greatest periods, where again, as at the beginning of the century, Wright was able to amalgamate the influences he had received with his own essentially unchanging objectives and principles and to produce thereby fresh masterpieces of his own.

One of the foremost among these was his Kaufmann House, "Falling Water," built across a stream called Bear Run, in Connellsville, Pennsylvania (plates 72, 74–76). "Falling Water" should be compared and contrasted not only with previous European work in general but specifically with the Lovell House, Los Angeles, built in 1929–30 by Richard Neutra, a Viennese architect of the International Style who had studied with Wright in the twenties (plate 73). Both houses step forward over depressions, but the Lovell House, with a few cantilevers, is essentially of rectangular steel frame construction, the classic fixation which Wright had always abhorred. "Falling Water" is of cantilever construction, the projecting slabs balanced on piers below and stabilized by the vertical masonry planes from which they spring. Their tan finished concrete sets off the darkness of the voids between them and contrasts with the tightly packed thin layers of the rough stone courses. The groupings of planes and their intersections are as crisply rectangular and articulated as any De Stijl project or as a painting by Mondrian (plate 55)—or as those of the Gale House (plate 38)—and the plan is as much a dance pattern of separate wall planes as anything by Mies (plate 56). In it, at last, the interior cave is truly fixed in the rock and opens out to the pavilion above the water. At once exploiting the most advanced structural techniques and fully celebrating the drama of nature's flow, "Falling Water" has always been rightfully considered one of the complete masterpieces of twentieth-century art. It too unites contemporary America and Europe, but it does more than this. A further comparison of it with the Lovell House, for example, will show that its superior plastic force derives partly from its essentially pyramidal composition. Compared now with Mayan temple renderings and with the Barnsdall House (plates 61, 62), "Falling Water" shows that Wright had finally found how to use the Mayan pyramid and its strong horizontal shadow lines in creative terms which were structurally and spatially integral rather than picturesquely derivative.

By 1937, with the Herbert Jacobs House (plates 77–79), Wright had created his first "Usonian" house type, his suburban (read, ideally, agrarian) answer to Le Corbusier's urban Citrohans (plate 65). The spaces, laid out in a rectangular module on a "floated" (no real footings) concrete slab with hot water pipes laid in it, may owe something to European plans, but the essentials are Wright's own. The central fireplace mass, housing the utilities within it, rises at the intersection of the two axes of living room pavilion and lower bedroom wing. The exterior wall is of wood sandwich construction, with all posts ("have no posts, no columns") eliminated except at the ranges of French doors. Finished simply but warmly inside and out with its own structural wood and brick, and built very cheaply, the house extended Wright's Broadacre City concept into the realm of feasible small house building and was, at its own scale, as intrinsic a work as "Falling Water." It too marked a kind of climax in the long contemporary search, both American and European, for a reasonable and expressive dwelling-house form.

Immediately Wright attempted to integrate that form further by uniting the almost inevitable "tail" of bedrooms more fully with the main volumes of the house. One method toward this out of which many houses grew was what Wright called the "reflex" one, of the hexagonal module. This, as in the Hanna House of 1937 (plates 80, 81), allowed a more truly fluid association of spaces and was thus exactly in the line of Wright's endless search for "eternal becoming." With it, too, the play of interior light becomes even richer and more plastic. Certainly from the time of the Jacobs and Hanna houses Wright's use of the module as a form creator, always implicit in his work, became more obsessive but extraordinarily supple. The Vigo Sundt Project of 1942, as well as many others, used the hexagonal system to create a spatial envelope essentially triangular and thereby more compact than the running hexagons of the Hanna House (plate 82).

Through all these experiments in spatial continuity and abstract control Wright never entirely abandoned the rectangular module, nor did he ever entirely lose sight of European achievements. His Goetsch-Winkler House of 1939 attempted to conceal the difficult bedroom "tail" by drawing it, on the entrance side, into planar continuity with the main living area (plates 83–85). The result more than a little resembles the composition of the Barcelona Pavilion (plate 58). But the interior space is entirely different, an engulfing volume, lighted by clerestories, and stabilized by the fireplace mass (plate 85). Wright remained, too, more sculpturally aggressive than the Europeans were at that period. His sculpture has the double quality of seeming almost solid and yet being fully expressive of his deeper consideration, the hollow of interior space. The Lloyd Lewis House of 1940 is an excellent embodiment of this expressive union (plates 86–88).

Its two-storied plan recalls Wright's first Willey project of 1932, which had at that time to be revised into a more conservative though highly successful one-storied version. Entrance under the raised living floor of the Lewis House and movement up out of the darkness to the expansive openness of the living room is again an emotional progress in space and light, as in all of Wright's buildings: from very low to higher, from compression to release, from dark to light. One of the most sculptural of the Usonians was the Rose Pauson House, built in the desert near Phoenix, Arizona, in 1940 and since burned, leaving only its great concrete piers, with their aggregate of massive desert stones, standing as monumental sentinels on the hill (plates 89, 90). The densely-lapped wooden siding of the projected balconies, carried on steel, was woven around the concrete masses. The entrance to the house, reached by a long, straight, cross axial path up the hill, was under them and between the piers and led into the two-storied living room. The interior hollow did not vitiate the exterior mass, which could thus stand solid in relation to the mountain forms which were its complement.

In the desert, during the thirties, Wright found his ideal place at last. From 1938 onward, until his death there in April, 1959, Taliesin West, not far from Phoenix, Arizona, was his favored home (plates 91–96). Here he was able to go deeper even than the Jeffersonian setting at Spring Green had enabled him to do: deeper than white America, turning "his back on white society," as Lawrence, also coming to live in the western desert, had written of the characteristic American hero a decade before.[38] At the new Taliesin Wright gathered his family and apprentices around him like some Apache chief and made use of the poured concrete and desert stone in forms which recall those of the Valley of Mexico rather than the softer and more civil shapes of Mayan work. Like a chief, he celebrated the oasis which he held and dragged heraldic boulders from the desert to announce his place. More than this, at Taliesin West Wright came to the heart of the American myth, to the wholly empty land beyond civilization, to the sea of naked earth, beyond Cooper's "sea of trees" and "sea of grass." Here was, in a sense, the objective of all mobility, all "getting away." So in its plan—defined both by its hard-shadowed, concrete masses and by their opposite in the spread, tent-like canvas ceiling —the movement is directed along a strong set of axes and reflex diagonals like an abstracted dry river of space. It runs behind the great redwood trusses of the drafting room, cut off from the desert, until at last the building mass splits and the desert is seen again, empty and vast, now framed and given dimension by the architectural forms. To the left was Wright's own two-winged Usonian house, enclosed in a secret green garden against the emptiness and with its own fire deep in its heart. Behind, however, exactly on the cross axis toward the empty space, rises the great gullied mass of a mountain, which spreads its arms around the encampment below it. The movement toward the continuity of landscape space is thus stabilized and given its opposite by the fixed, looming, and protecting mountain form. It is a fact that all Cretan palace sites directed the main axes of their central courtyards exactly toward a sacred mountain peak, which contained a cave shrine of the Minoan goddess of the earth. The sacred mountains were invariably cleft and horned, a good deal like Wright's mountain here.[39] The special resemblance of Phaistos to Wright's use of the mountain mass seems especially cogent, since there Ida rises "behind" the courtyard (plate 97) which otherwise opens southward to a valley view. It is clear that Wright always knew and admired Cretan architecture, since the first publications of it by Evans, which appeared from the end of the nineteenth century onward throughout Wright's earlier years.[40] Its full subservience to the shapes of the earth, and the flowing, curvilinear continuities of its art, celebrating as they did the continuous rhythms of the earth and its goddess, must always have been sympathetic to him, although he had previously left their exploitation to the Art Nouveau architects of his youth.

But it was exactly at this period in his life, when he finally fixed his palace under the mountain, that dominant curves first began to play a major part in Wright's architectural design. The first and perhaps the finest of this series was the Johnson Wax Company Office Building, at Racine, Wisconsin, of 1936–39 (plates 98–101). It may be too much to suggest that its "lily pad" concrete columns were directly inspired by Minoan "table leg" columns as they are known from gems and frescoes and as they were reconstructed by Evans at Knossos. Yet the point of the Cretan column is precisely that it rises between walls, rarely outside them, and if so, framed by them. Indeed the column flanked, whether by walls or by lions as at Mycenae, was the goddess herself. The horned shrines of the goddess thus used their columns as sacred objects essentially inside, encased by the wall planes (plate 102), exactly as Wright used them in the great room of the Johnson Wax Building[41] (plate 101). Here too Wright dramatized the transfiguration to be gained through engulfment by the goddess, a concept also central to Minoan-Mycenaean religion. Therefore the exterior walls are expressed as non-bearing, i.e., as purely for enclosure, and they rush in strong curves toward the low, dark entrance, where the columns are compressed, as at the entrance to a cave (plate 100). Beyond this dark place, however, the shafts rise up swelling to their full height and receive the light which filters down through the glass tubing above them (plate 101). They thus stand as if growing and floating in the quietest place of all, a deep and limpid pool. In that way they also recall the open papyrus columns of Egyptian hypostyle halls. To this most compelling of images Wright later added its complement, in the deeply tap-rooted laboratory tower of 1950 (plate 103). This in its clarity is a true successor of St. Mark's Tower, and it completes the powerfully abstract massing of the Johnson Wax exterior.

Clearly enough, from this time onward for the rest of his life, Wright was keenly aware of the principles of the non-Greek Mediterranean architectural tradition. His plan of 1938 for Florida Southern College would seem to have derived its pivotal circular pool, its long opening and closing diagonal axes with their colonnades, perhaps even its outdoor theatre and top-lighted buildings of many shapes—such as the chapel and the library—from the published plans of Hadrian's Villa at Tivoli, of the early second century A. D. (plates 104, 105). Wright's details in concrete and concrete blocks are Mayoid rather than Roman, as is his scale, but the analogy of Wright with Hadrian is a good one. Both were men who lived in late phases of a long cultural period, who deeply felt the fluxes and changes which time brought to human life, and who therefore sought to find deep and stable roots for their experience and psychic comfort for themselves in old traditions. Hadrian had also looked into the pre-Hellenic past, and some of his buildings at the Villa, such as the great dining room and the Serapieion, were obviously meant to recall the engulfing shapes of the ancient Mediterranean religion of the goddess of the earth.[42] Late projects by Wright, consciously or unconsciously, do exactly this also. The Ralph Jester (Martin Pence) Project of 1930–40 (plate 107) makes purely rounded enclosures to be built either of plywood, masonry, or concrete. Some were to have been lighted only from above. It is the hollow that counts here, and its shape recalls the constructed megalithic caverns in the form of the goddess herself which were built on prehistoric Malta (plate 108). Such caverns had no exterior form, and Wright's exteriors in this vein are pure expressions of the interior hollow. He often stated his intention clearly—holding up the cylinder of a water glass and, citing Lao-Tse, stating that its "reality" was the space inside. In terms that would have been understood by ancient man, he then called that interior the place of "great Peace."[43] Water itself, enclosed by the circle, played an archetypal part in many of these designs, as it had done for Hadrian as well (plate 109).

Many projects by Wright then explored the curve, its continuities, and its engulfments. The Second Jacobs House, finally built in 1948, is an excellent example (plates 110–112). Dug into the earth on the north side, like the Maltese shrines and the sod huts of prairie pioneers alike, it opens southward in a curving sweep which houses all the units of living space integrally within it. Its arc partly encloses a deep earth hollow, and it sends its overhangs out to pick up the continuities of the prairie horizon. Wright's house of 1952 for his son, David, sends the curve up in a continuous spiral (plate 113) like those labyrinth symbols which are also to be found carved in Megalithic temples and tombs. In the Morris Store, of 1948–49, the spiral is enclosed within the building shell and is lighted by a female ceiling (plates 114, 115). The facade of Roman brick is pierced only by a round-headed opening which recalls, here toward the end of Wright's life, the engulfing arches of Richardson (plate 3)—as the brick recalls McKim, Mead and White and the Charnley and Winslow houses (plates 8, 10, 11).

These two compelling movements—the first, toward immurement in the ideal hollow, and the second (deeply traditional also but now Nietzschean-heroic in its force) toward the conquest of time itself through the use of the continuous spiral, "beyond time and infinity," which returns cyclically and never seems to end—are climaxed in the Guggenheim Museum of 1946–59 (plates 116–120). Here it was purely these mystical drives which formed the design. Many of the details and intersections of the Museum as finally executed are awkward and even gross, mirroring a kind of impatience, perhaps, at the last, haste. The domed and spiralling space is the whole, causing the building to balloon outward among its starched neighbors, like the pulsing sanctuary of a primitive cult drumming on Fifth Avenue. For this reason the concrete, which seemed so muscular while the structure was under way and which is so structurally suited to the form, was given its rather metallic coat of tan paint—in order to take weight off the solids and let the "space," not the "matter," become the whole "reality."

Much has been made of the problem of installation faced by the museum's director, who had the difficult job of trying to make objects of art appear as special and separate entities in a Wright building. Yet, once the design was accepted as a museum (a decision of doubtful wisdom), it may be that the authorities would have been well advised to follow Wright's intentions through to the letter. The present solution of projecting the pictures far into the ramp on metal bars, of painting the walls and ceiling around them white, and of installing fluorescent lights in Wright's clerestories and in the ceilings as well, not only does the pictures little good but severely injures the building itself by substituting a department-store harshness of glare—compressive upon the space—for the naturally changing and expansive light that the ramps demand. Even Wright's proposal to lean the paintings far back on shelves against the outer wall and under the natural light, would have been kinder to the individual pictures, since their backward slant as so installed would have compensated in part for the downward slope of the ramp which makes it so difficult at present for the visitor to focus upon them.

The building as a whole offers many strange and significant effects. Upon entrance, under the skeletally obtrusive and therefore volume-negating dome, the building seems small. It does not exalt man standing fixed and upright within it. The meaning is in the journey, since from above, upon leaving the elevator, the visitor finds the space dizzying and vast, while the great downward coil of the ramp insistently invites him to movement. Upon arriving at the ground floor once more, he will find that the building seems much larger than before because the long journey through it is remembered. But as that memory fades, the heavy vertical piers (not, as in the Larkin Building, intrinsic to the spatial experience but counter to it), the dome struts, and the bright side-lights catch his eye and reduce the space in size once more, so that he must move again soon if the sensation of freedom and vastness is to be regained. Thus he is kept, in all truth, "on the road."

In these ways Wright, toward the close of his long, difficult, and courageous life, used all the images he had grown up with or could find in order to give satisfactory form to the feeling of change and the wish for belonging which were deep in the American mind. In his own way, and in accordance with his own different reading of the past, Wright's greatest rival, Le Corbusier, has been doing exactly the same thing during his later decades.[44] Thus Wright's circles were in part his escape from "International" pressure, and his nineteenth-century imagery took on new life as well. So his Unitarian Church, at Madison, Wisconsin, of 1947, is both plow and ship, biting into the prairie like something moving forward (plates 121–123). Its choir is raised up behind the glass and under the "praying hands" of the roof, like the suspended pulpit, reached by a rope ladder drawn up behind, in which Melville's New Bedford parson preached of whales.

Some of the late imagery is fevered. The mounting spiral of the "Golden Triangle" Project for Pittsburgh, of 1947, was finally called a "ziggurat" and used to form avenues and parking areas for the Arabian Night's dream of mountains, water, and shimmering surfaces which Wright so gustily imagined for Bagdad (plate 124). Finally, like the peoples of the Ancient East, Wright built his own sacred mountain. He tells us that the dauntless rabbi who commissioned the Beth Sholom Synagogue at Elkins Park, Pennsylvania, in 1959, suggested that he create a "traveling Mount Sinai" in glass, a "mountain of light."[45] How the congregation interpreted the conflicting passages in *Psalms* and *Jeremiah* concerning the utility and propriety of sacred mountains was its own affair. What Wright gave them was the cone of Astarte in her horned enclosure at Byblos, as known from a coin of the Emperor Macrinus and published by Evans in his "Mycenaean Tree and Pillar Cult," of 1901[46] (plates 125, 126).

Except for the horns of its buttresses, the synagogue also recalls the Lake Tahoe and Nakoma tepees of the early twenties (plate 67). It is Cezanne's Mont Sainte Victoire as well (plate 42). Therefore it hardly matters whether Wright knew of Byblos or not. He instinctively went to the tradition which meant most to him, that of the sanctity of the earth and of its female forms. But as the sort of modern, or late nineteenth-century man he was, he somehow had to overstep the old Hellenic boundaries between nature and the human will and to seek to do more than had been done before and to direct the whole of things himself, if he could. So in one of his last projects, that for the Civic Center of Marin County, California, the long superimposed arcades, almost like Roman aqueducts, stretch out to grasp the rounded hills above the automobile traffic which rushes and flows below them (plate 127). The conical summit of the central hill is leveled off, and Wright sets his own glass-domed cone top upon it. In front of this a thin tower is raised, like a ship's tall mast, and a long prow divides the hill, saiiing onward.

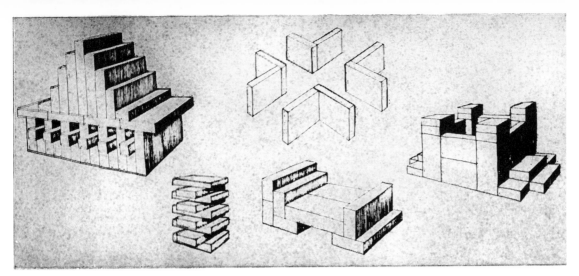

1. Froebel constructions. (Drawn by Grant Manson)

2. "Planter's House" (E. C. Gardner's *Illustrated Homes,* 1875)

3. Crane Memorial Library, Quincy, Massachusetts, 1880–83, by Henry Hobson Richardson.

4. Kent House, Tuxedo Park, New York, 1885–86, by Bruce Price.

5. Kent House. Plan.

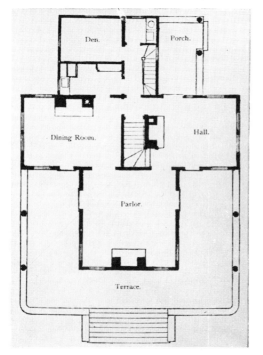

6. F. L. Wright House, Oak Park, Illinois, 1889.

7. F. L. Wright House. Interior.

8. House, New York, 1887, by McKim, Mead, and White.

9. Wainwright Building, St. Louis, Missouri, 1890–91, by Louis Sullivan.

0. Charnley House, Chicago, Illinois, 1891.

11. Winslow House, River Forest, Illinois, 1893. Street facade.

12. Winslow House. Plan.

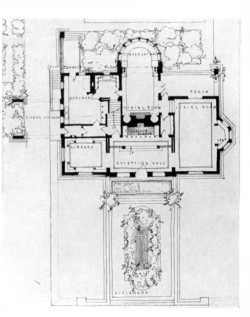

13. Winslow House. Rear view.

14. Husser House, Chicago, Illinois, 1899.

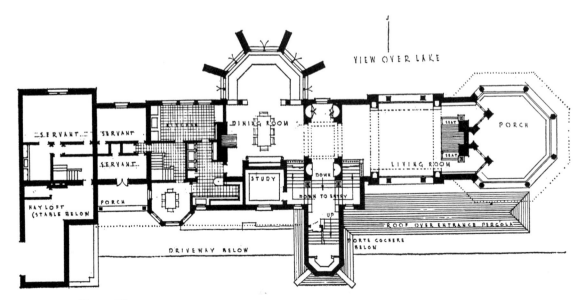

15. Husser House. Plan.

16. "Romeo and Juliet" windmill, Spring Green, Wisconsin, 1896. First shingled, later boarded and battened.

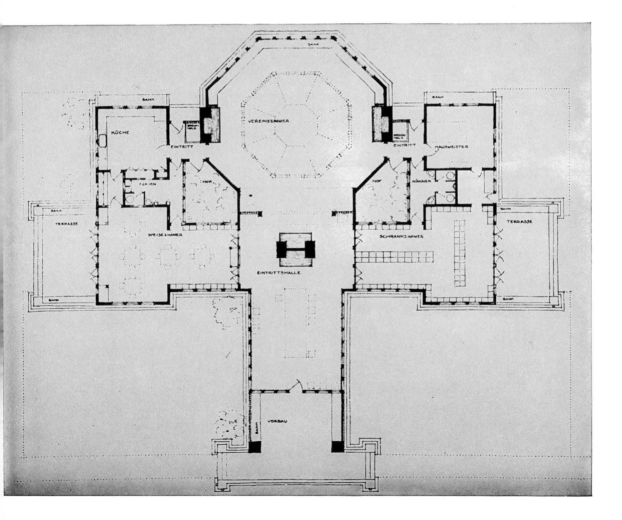

19. Ward Willitts House, Highland Park, Illinois, 1900(?)–02.

20. Ward Willitts House. **Plan.**

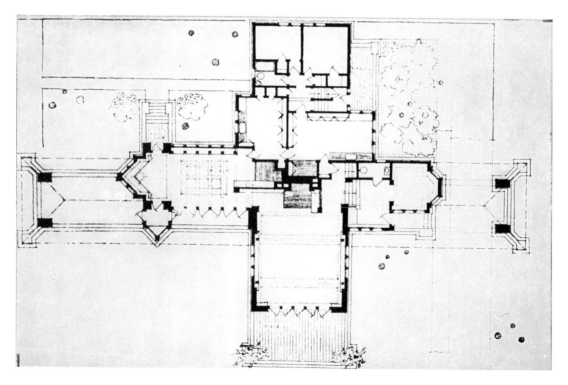

21. Ho-o-Den, Imperial Japanese Exhibit, Chicago, 1893. Plan (drawn by Grant Manson) and view.

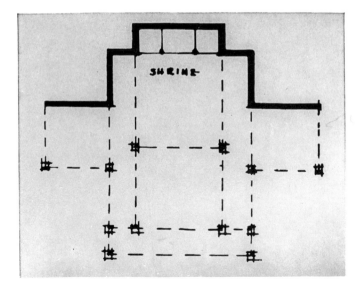

22. Villa Rotunda, Vicenza, 1560, by Andrea Palladio. Plan, Section, Elevation Drawing.

23. Heurtley House, Chicago, Illinois, 1902.

24. Heurtley House. Living Room.

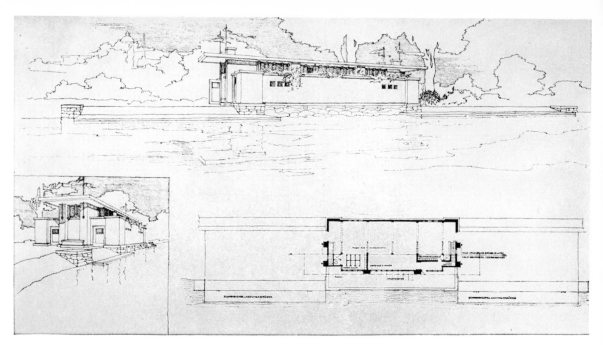

25. Yahara Boat Club Project, 1902.

26. Martin House, Buffalo, New York, 1904.

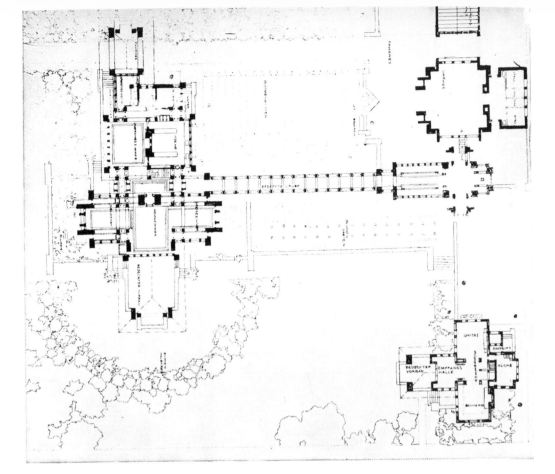

27. Martin House. Plan.

28. Martin House. Living Room.

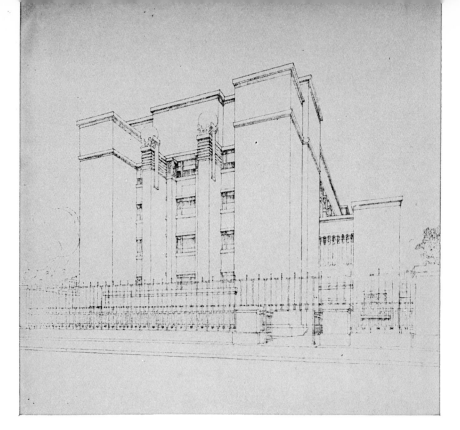

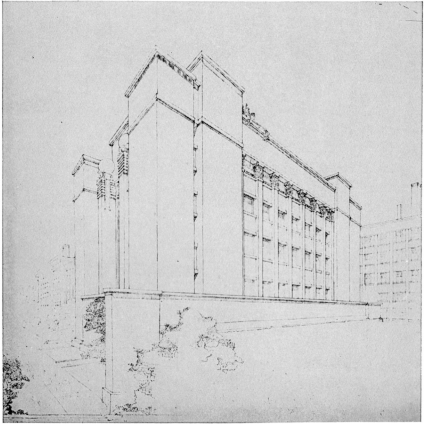

29, 30. Larkin Building, Buffalo, New York, 1904. Destroyed 1950. Perspective drawing (above), perspective drawing with entrance (below).

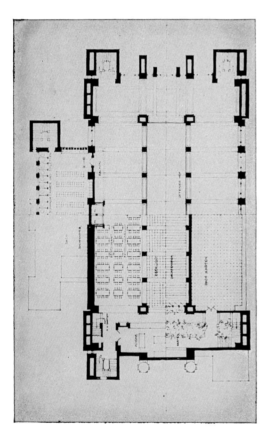

31. Larkin Building. Plan.

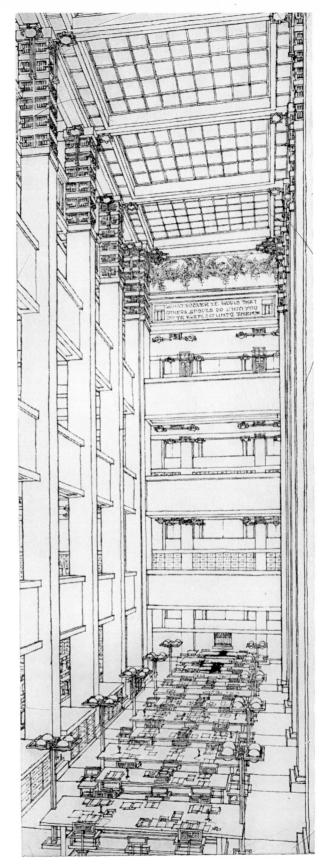

32. Larkin Building. Interior. Drawing.

33. Unity Church. Oak Park, Illinois, 1906.

34. Unity Church. Plan.

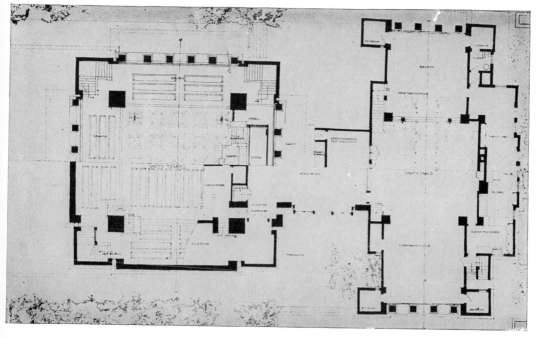

35. Unity Church. Interior.

36. Coonley House, Riverside, Illinois, 1908. Interior, looking toward living room.

37. Roberts House, River Forest, Illinois, 1908. Living room.

38. Gale House, Oak Park, Illinois, 1909.

39. Robie House, Chicago, Illinois, 1909.

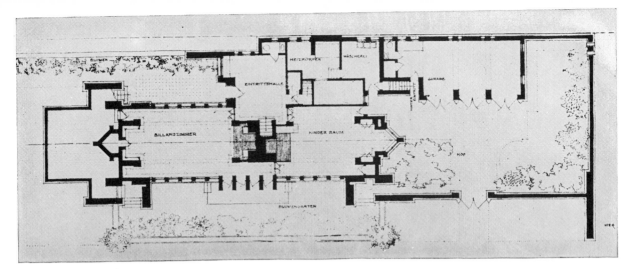

40. Robie House. Plan.

41. Robie House. Oblique view.

42. Quarry and Mont Sainte Victoire, 1898–1900, by Paul Cézanne.

43. Guitarist, 1914, by Georges Braque.

44. Taliesin I, Spring Green, Wisconsin, 1911. Roofs and Court.

45. Taliesin I. Court and Entrance Loggia.

46. Taliesin III. Living Room.

47. Coonley Playhouse, Riverside, Illinois, 1912. Exterior.

48. Coonley Playhouse. Plan.

49. Midway Gardens, Chicago, Illinois, 1914.

50. Midway Gardens. Detail.

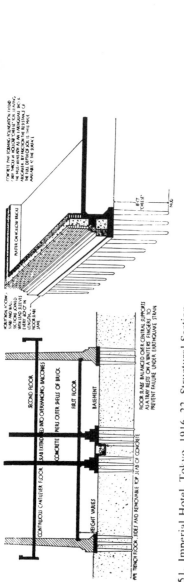

51. Imperial Hotel. Tokyo, 1916–22. Structural Section.

52. Imperial Hotel. Lobby.

53. Imperial Hotel. Courtyard.

54. Ward Willitts House, 1902. Side View.

55. Painting #1, 1921, by Piet Mondrian. Basel, collection Müller-Widmann.

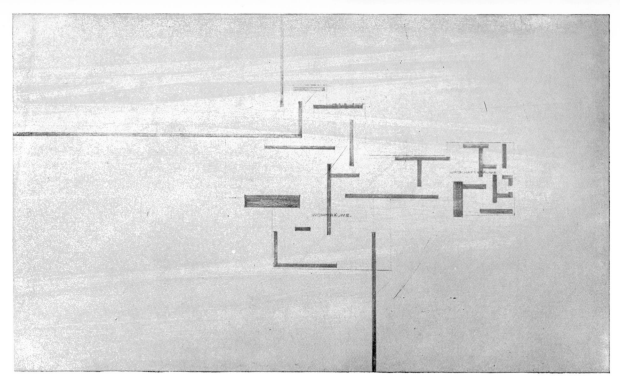

56. Project for a Brick Country House, 1923, by Ludwig Mies Van der Rohe. Plan.

57. Walter Gerts House, Glencoe, Illinois, 1906. Plan.

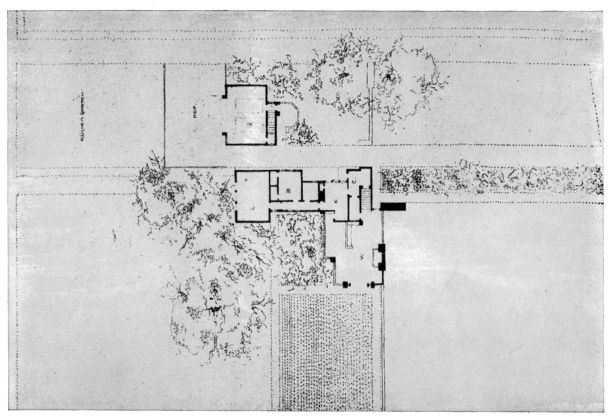

58. German Pavilion, International Exposition, Barcelona, 1929, by Mies Van der Rohe.

59. A. D. German Warehouse, Richland Center, Wisconsin, 1915.

60. Temple of the Two Lintels, Chichen Itza, Yucatan.

61. Barnsdall House, Hollywood, California, 1920.

62. Structure 33, Yaxchilan. Restoration after Bolles.

63. Millard House, Pasadena, California, 1923. Perspective Drawing.

64. Millard House.

65. Citrohan House Project, 1922, by Le Corbusier. Model.

66. Freeman House, Los Angeles, California, 1924. Living Room.

67. Lake Tahoe Summer Colony Project, 1922. Shore Type Cabin.

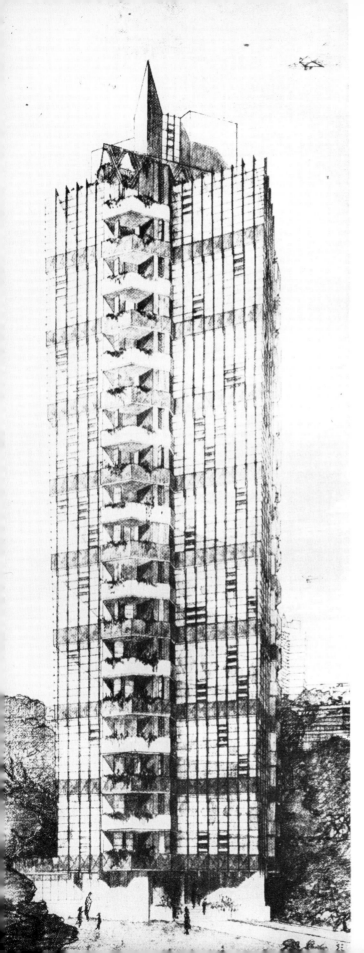

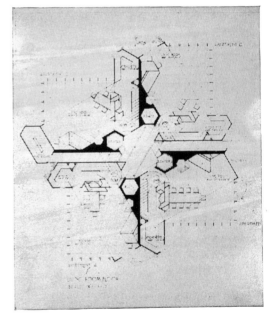

69. St. Mark's Tower. Plan.

68. St. Mark's Tower, New York, Project, 1929.

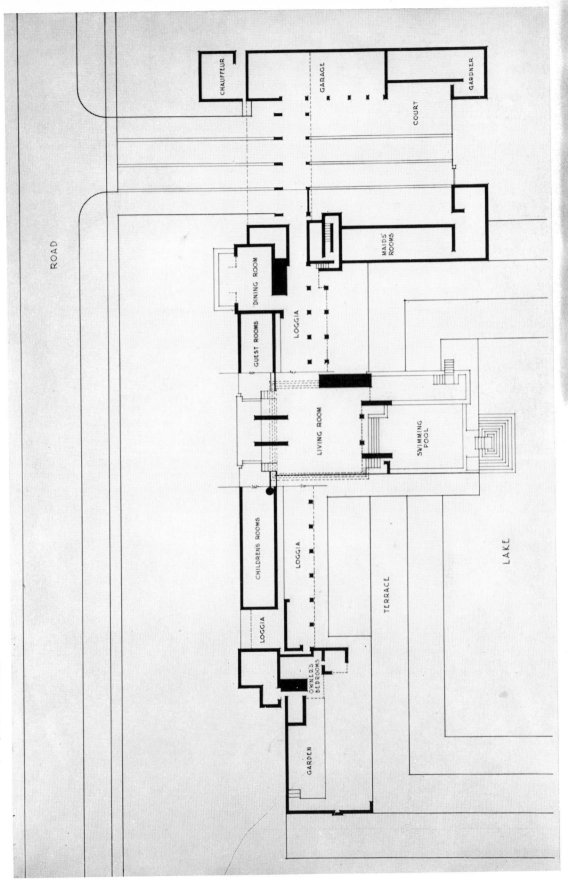

70. Broadacre City, Project, c. 1931–1935 (opposite).

71. House on the Mesa, Project, 1932. Plan.

72. Kaufmann House, "Falling Water," Connellsville, Pennsylvania, 1936–37. View from entrance bridge.

73. Lovell House, Los Angeles, California, 1929–30, by Richard Neutra.

74. Kaufmann House. From below.

75. Kaufmann House. Detail.

76. Kaufmann House. Plan.

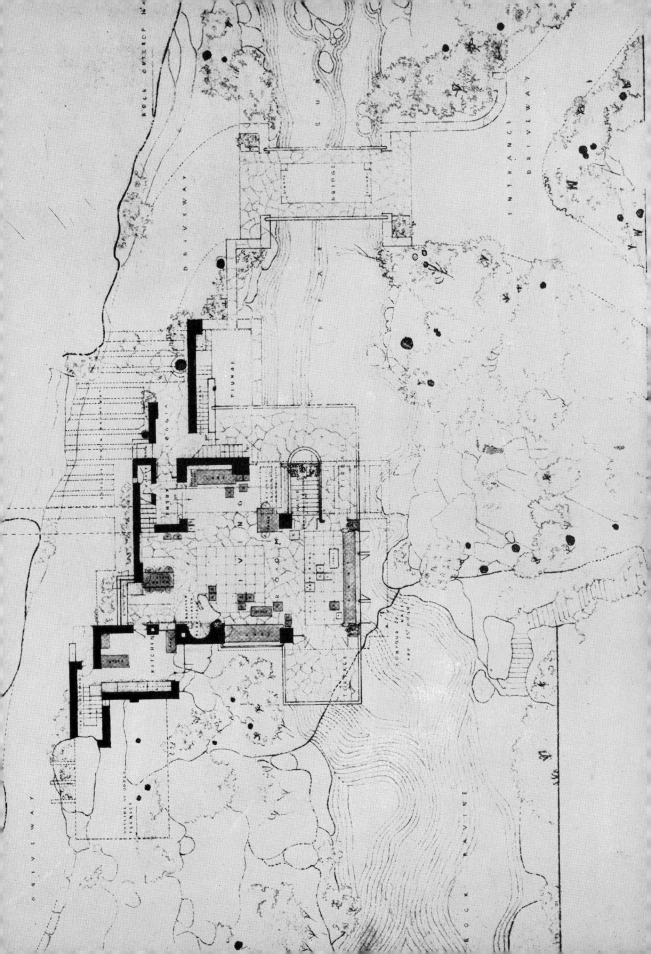

77. First Herbert Jacobs House, Madison, Wisconsin, 1937.

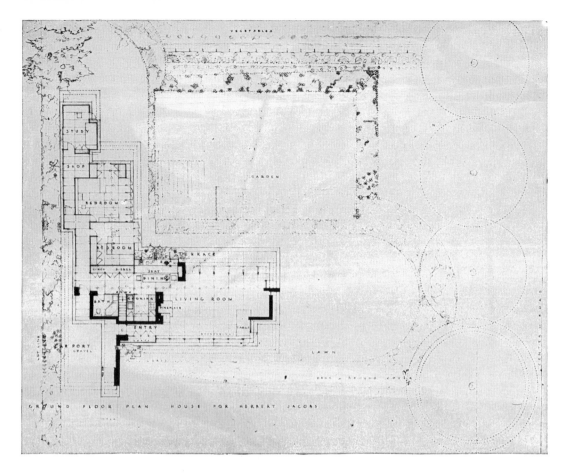

78. First Jacobs House. Plan.

79. First Jacobs House. Living Room.

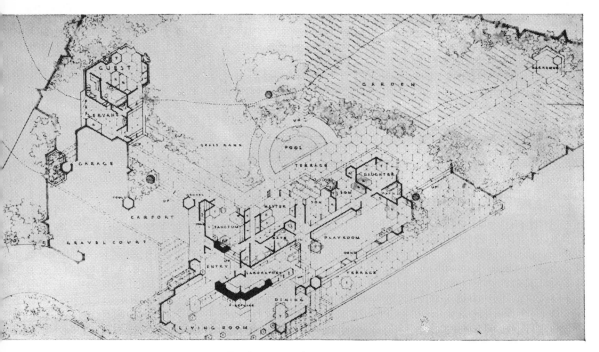

80. Hanna House, Palo Alto, California, 1937. Plan.

81. Hanna House. Living Room.

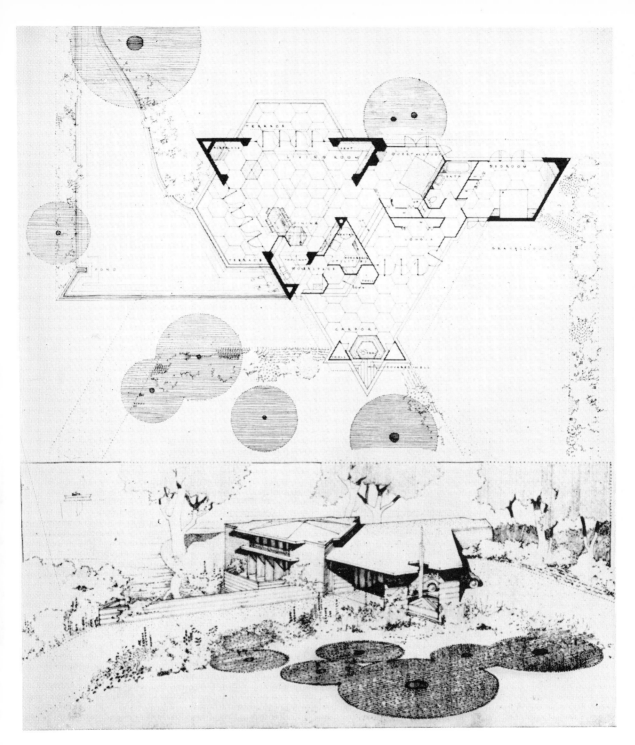

82. Vigo Sundt House, Madison, Wisconsin. Project of 1942. Plan and Perspective.

83. Goetsch-Winkler House, Okemos, Michigan, 1939. Entrance Front.

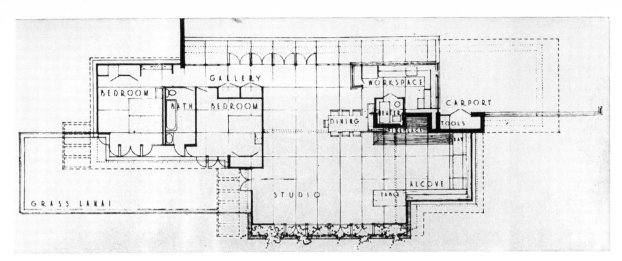

84. Goetsch-Winkler House. Plan.

85. Goetsch-Winkler House. Living Room.

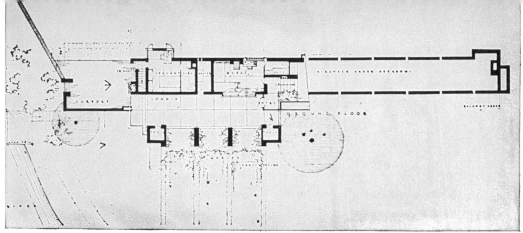

86. Lloyd Lewis House, Libertyville, Illinois, 1940. Plan.

87. Lloyd Lewis House. Entrance.

88. Lloyd Lewis House. Living Room.

89. Pauson House, Phoenix, Arizona, 1940. Rear view.

90. Pauson House. Entrance side. Entrance in center. Living Room far end.

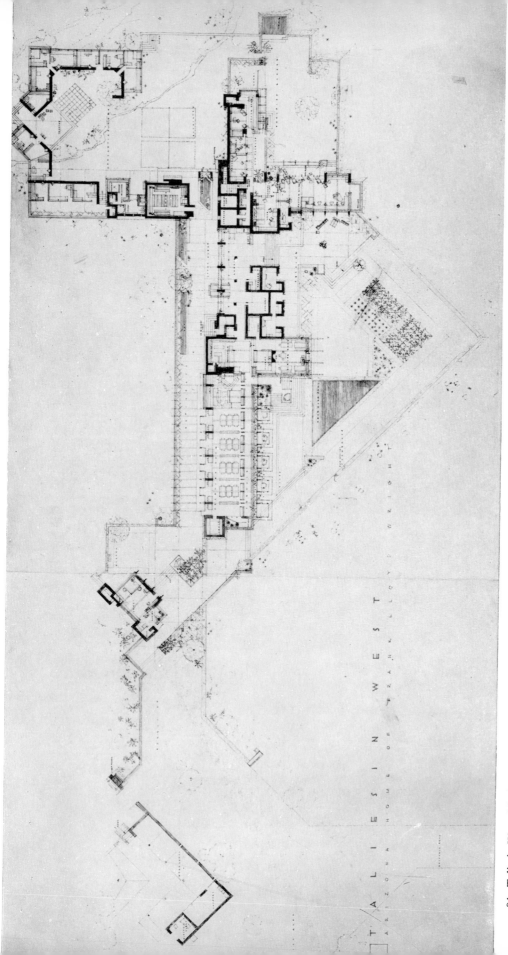

91. Taliesin West, Maricopa Mesa, near Phoenix, Arizona, 1938–1959. Plan.

92. Taliesin West. Pool. House. Mountain.

93. Taliesin West. View along platform behind drafting room.

94. Taliesin West.

95. Taliesin West. Wright's living quarters with their court.

96. Taliesin West. Showing axis of desert, loggia, mountain.

97. The Palace at Phaistos, Crete. Axis of the courtyard with Mount Ida.

98. Johnson Wax Administration Building, Racine, Wisconsin, 1936–39, 1950.

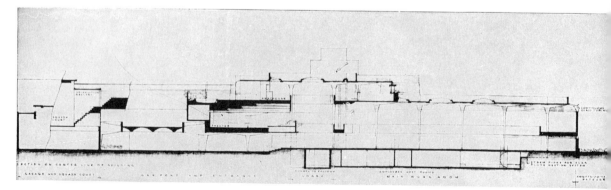

99. Johnson Wax Building. Section.

100. Johnson Wax Building. Entrance.

101. Johnson Wax Building. Interior.

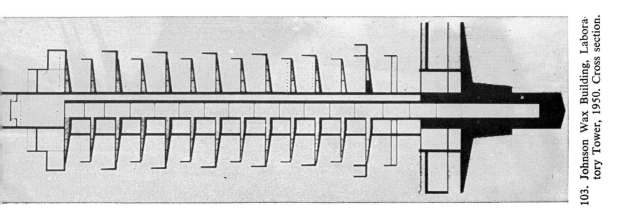

103. Johnson Wax Building, Laboratory Tower, 1950. Cross section.

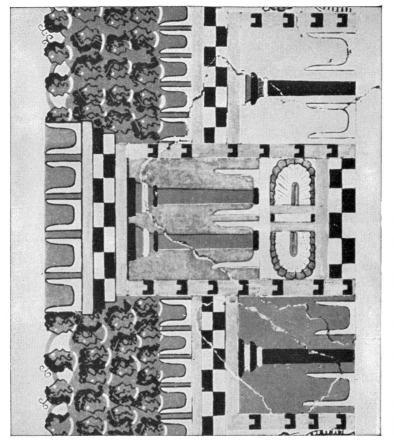

102. Knossos, Crete. Fresco of the goddess' shrine.

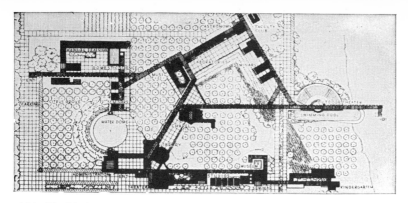

104. Florida Southern College, Lakeland, Florida, 1938–1959. Plan.

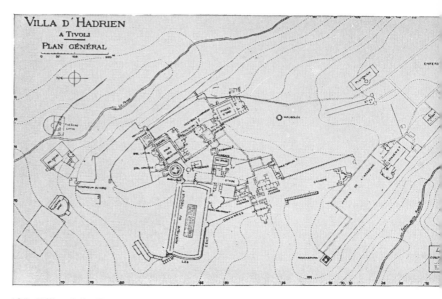

105. Villa of the Emperor Hadrian, Tivoli. Plan. (After Kähler)

106. Florida Southern College. Colonnades and Chapel.

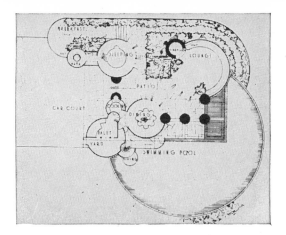

107. Ralph Jester (Martin Pence) Project, 1938 (1940). Plan.

108. Megalithic Temples, Malta. View of model from above. (After Zammit)

109. Villa of the Emperor Hadrian, Tivoli, "Teatro Marittimo." Island Pavilion. (After Kähler)

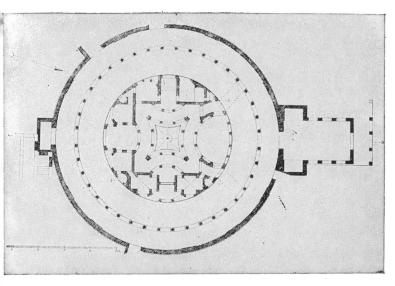

110. Second Jacobs House, Madison, Wisconsin, 1948. North, entrance side.

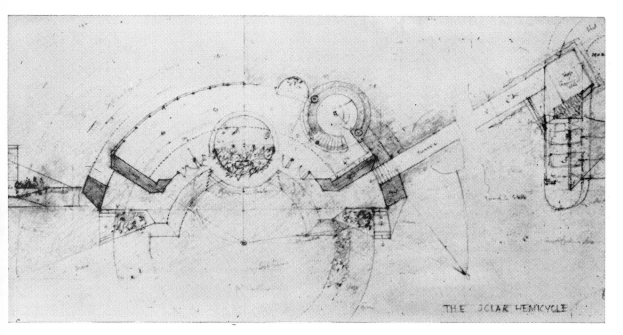

THE SOLAR HEMICYCLE

111. Second Jacobs House. Plan.

112. Second Jacobs House. Interior.

113. David Wright House, Phoenix, Arizona, 1952.

114. Morris Gift Shop, San Francisco, California, 1948–49. Exterior.

115. Morris Gift Shop. Interior.

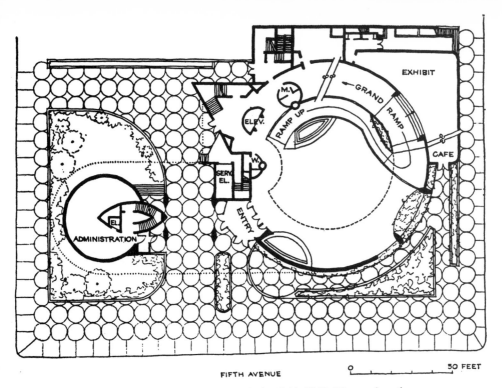

FIFTH AVENUE

0   50 FEET

116. Solomon R. Guggenheim Museum, New York, 1946–1959. Plan and section.

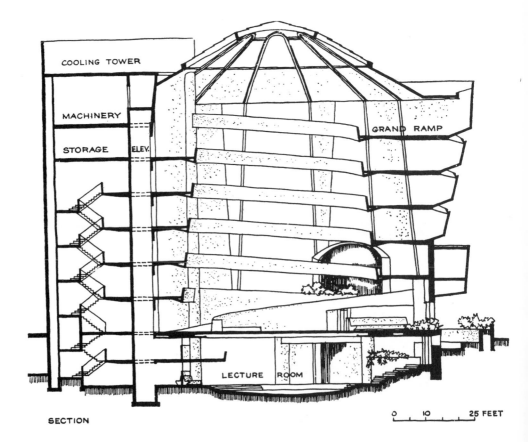

SECTION

0   10   25 FEET

17. Guggenheim Museum. Interior.

118. Guggenheim Museum. The Dome.

119. Guggenheim Museum. Spirals.

120. Guggenheim Museum. Exterior.

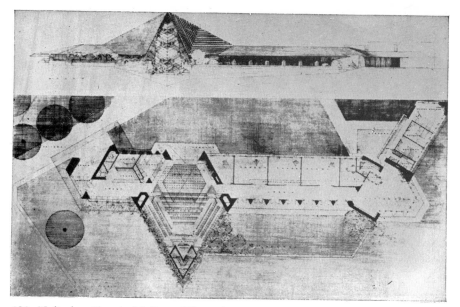

121. Unitarian Church, Madison, Wisconsin, 1947. Plan and Elevation.

122. Unitarian Church. The Prow.

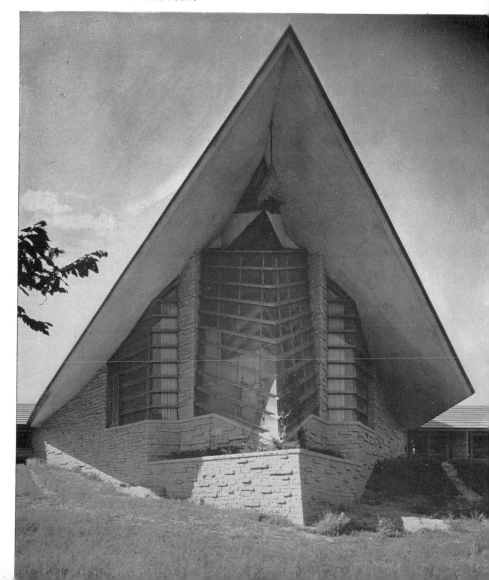

3. Unitarian Church. Interior looking toward choir.

124. Project for Grand Opera and Civic Auditorium, Bagdad, Iraq, 1957.

5. Beth Sholom Synagogue, Elkins Park, Pennsylvania, 1959.

126. Cone of Astarte in her horned enclosure at Byblos.

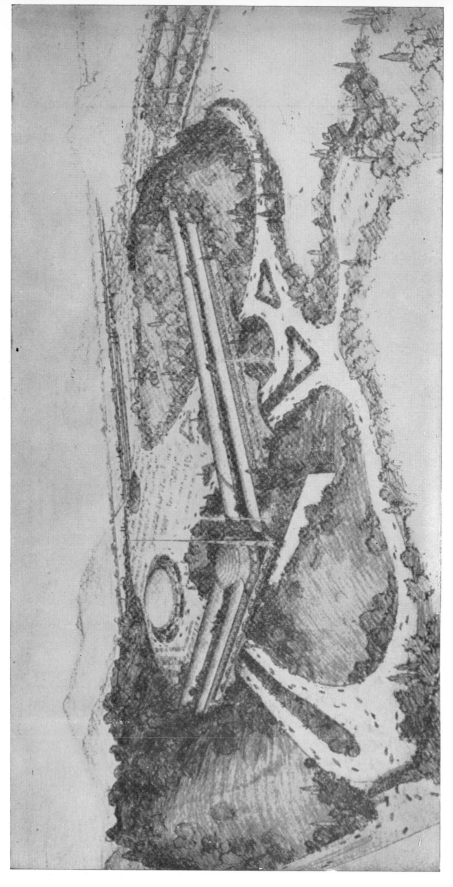

127. Civic Center for Marin County, California, 1959.

NOTES

1. Published in: Frank Lloyd Wright, *An Organic Architecture: The Architecture of Democracy*, London, 1939. See also *idem, The Future of Architecture*, New York, 1953, p. 242.
2. *Idem,* "The Language of Organic Architecture," *Architectural Forum,* May, 1953, p. 106.
3. Quoted by Wright: *Architectural Forum,* January, 1938, p. 37.
4. Cf. W. H. Auden, *The Enchafèd Flood; or, The Romantic Iconography of the Sea,* New York, 1950. Albert Camus, *L'Homme Révolté,* Paris, 1951.
5. Sybil Moholy-Nagy, "Frank Lloyd Wright's Testament," *College Art Journal,* XVIII, 4, p. 321.
6. Cf. Donald Drew Egbert, "The Idea of Organic Expressionism and American Architecture," in *Evolutionary Thought in America,* ed. Stowe Persons, New Haven, 1950, pp. 336–396.
7. G. C. Manson, *Frank Lloyd Wright to 1910, The First Golden Age,* New York, 1958, pp. 5–10.
8. *Ibid.,* figs. 2, 3.
9. Cf. V. J. Scully, *The Shingle Style, Architectural Theory and Design from Richardson to the Origins of Wright,* New Haven, 1955, pp. 19–33.
10. *Idem,* "Romantic-Rationalism and the Expression of Structure in Wood. Downing, Wheeler, Gardner and the 'Stick Style,' 1840–1876," *Art Bulletin,* 35, 1953, pp. 121–142.
11. Frank Lloyd Wright, *An Autobiography,* New York, 1943, p. 75. Later statements in the text about Wright's life are usually based upon the *Autobiography* and will not be footnoted.
12. *The Shingle Style,* pp. 126–129, 159, figs. 108–110, 155, 156.
13. *Ibid.,* figs. 114, 115, 121–125.
14. *Ibid.,* pp. 113–154.
15. Cf. Henry-Russell Hitchcock, "Frank Lloyd Wright and the 'Academic Tradition,'" *Journal of the Warburg and Courtauld Institutes,* 7, 1944, pp. 46–63.
16. *The Shingle Style,* figs. 98, 101. The Husser plan is already much more decisive and abstract than those by Eyre.
17. Manson, *op. cit.,* p. 93. Hitchcock was not puzzled and refers to this building as "a beacon pointing toward that ultimate marriage of engineering and architecture which we find in Wright's major works of the twentieth century..." Henry-Russell Hitchcock, *In the Nature of Materials. The Buildings of Frank Lloyd Wright, 1887–1941,* New York, 1942, p. 29.
18. For the Ho-o-den and others see: Clay Lancaster, "Japanese Buildings in the United States before 1900: Their Influence upon American Domestic Architecture," *Art Bulletin,* 35, 1953, pp. 217–224; pl. 9. This follows *idem,* "Oriental Forms in American Architecture, 1800–1870," *Art Bulletin,* 29, 1947, pp. 183–193. See also Manson, *op. cit.,* pp. 34–38.

19. Herman Melville, "I and My Chimney," as in *Selected Tales and Poems,* ed. by Richard Chase, New York, Rinehart, 7th printing, 1959, pp. 159–189.

20. *An Autobiography,* p. 141.

21. Some of the comments on *Huckleberry Finn* derive from Leslie A. Fiedler, "Come Back to the Raft Ag'in, Huck Honey!" in *An End to Innocence, Essays on Culture and Politics,* Boston, 1955, pp. 142–151. Also: the contrast between the Willitts House and the Villa Rotunda is not an arbitrarily chosen one. They are natural opposites, and had met before. That is, Jefferson's first plans for Monticello were cross-axial, with no central hollow and no dome, almost like the Price and Wright plans. He then stabilized his horizontality externally, though not internally, by a dome derived from Burlington's Chiswick, derived in turn from the Villa Rotunda. Thus the New World and the Old pulled at Jefferson. For Wright the Old World was dead. Cf. Fiske Kimball, *Thomas Jefferson, Architect,* Boston, 1916, figs. 5, 108 bis. Also: Clay Lancaster, "Jefferson's Architectural Indebtedness to Robert Morris," *JSAH,* 10, 1951, pp. 3–10, fig. 1.

22. These statements were made by Wright at many different times. They have been put together here from Edgar Kaufmann's useful edition of his writings, grouped by topic and illustrated. Frank Lloyd Wright, *An American Architecture,* New York, 1955, *passim.* Frederick Gutheim's earlier edition, arranged by date, is also a good source: *Frank Lloyd Wright On Architecture, Selected Writings 1894–1940,* New York, 1941. For Wright's best-connected statement of the process of invention in his early house designs, see, *An Autobiography,* pp. 139–150.

23. Louis I. Kahn, "Order in Architecture," *Perspecta, The Yale Architectural Journal,* 4, 1957, pp. 58–59.

24. As in designs by Boullée and Ledoux. Cf. Emil Kaufmann, "Three Revolutionary Architects, Boullee, Ledoux, and Lequeu," *Trans. American Philosophical Society,* 42, pt. 3, 1952, pp. 476–547. See also, *idem, Von Ledoux bis Le Corbusier; Ursprung und Entwicklung der Autonome Architektur,* Vienna and Leipzig, 1933. The Larkin Building also bares an extremely superficial resemblance to Olbrich's "Sezession" Building, in Vienna, of 1899. This may be why a few critics, inaccurately and with some malice, have occasionally referred to Wright's work as "Secession."

25. *An Autobiography,* pp. 153–160.

26. The phrase is from D. H. Lawrence's perceptive analysis of nineteenth-century American symbolism: *Studies in Classic American Literature,* London, 1922. Doubleday Anchor edition, New York, 1955, pp. 13 ff. Lawrence's own view of reality was itself reminiscent of Wright's.

27. This is another example of that unconscious community of formal invention toward 1910 that Giedion noted in his *Space, Time and Architecture,* Cambridge, revised edition, 1949, pp. 346, 367–382, and *passim.* I personally am not in agreement with Giedion's "space-time" analogy to physics and prefer the terms "fragmentation" and "continuity" to describe the art of this period. Cf. my "Modern Architecture: Toward a Redefinition of Style," *College Art Journal,* XVII, 2, 1958, pp. 140–159; reprinted in *Reflections on Art,* ed. by Susanne K. Langer, Baltimore, 1958, pp. 342–356.

28. *An Autobiography,* pp. 162–164.

29. The first consisted of plans and drawings: *Ausgeführte Bauten und Entwürfe von Frank Lloyd Wright,* Berlin, Ernst Wasmuth, 1910. The second published photographs and had an introduction by the English architect, C. R. Ashbee: *Frank Lloyd Wright: Ausgeführte Bauten,*

Berlin, Ernst Wasmuth, 1911. The publications were suggested to Wasmuth by Kuno Francke, Roosevelt Exchange Professor of Esthetics at Harvard. *An Autobiography*, pp. 161–162.

30. The Mason City Bank: *Ausgeführte Bauten und Entwürfe*, pls. 49, 49^2; the Yahara Boat Club: *ibid.*, pl. 55.

31. Cf. Piet Mondrian, *Plastic Art and Pure Plastic Art*, 3rd revised edition, New York, 1951, esp. pp. 42–43.

32. V. J. Scully, "Frank Lloyd Wright vs. the International Style," *Art News*, 53, March, 1954, pp. 32 ff. For various objections and my reply, see *op. cit.*, September, 1954, pp. 48–49.

33. Lawrence, *op. cit.*, pp. 44, 45.

34. D. T. Tselos, "Exotic Influences in the Architecture of Frank Lloyd Wright," *Magazine of Art*, 46, 1953, pp. 160–169.

35. This and other Mayan monuments were well published and available to Wright. For bibliography see, for example, Henry Joseph Spinden, *Maya Art and Civilization*, Indian Hills, 1957. There may, strangely, have been specifically Mayan influence upon some of Price's designs of 1885–86 at Tuxedo Park, which had influenced Wright at his beginning. Such seems possible from their forms, and Price's client, Pierre Lorillard, had just financed Charnay's expedition to the Mayan area and the publication of its results. Cf. D. Charnay, *Les Anciennes Villes du Nouveau Monde*, Paris, 1885.

36. *An Autobiography*, p. 147.

37. Cf. note 34, above.

38. Lawrence, *op. cit.*, p. 73. Lawrence lived in New Mexico at intervals from 1922 to 1925.

39. As Mt. Jouctas south of Knossos and Ida north of Phaistos. See also: L. Pernier, *Il Palazzo minoico di Festos*, I and II, Rome, 1935, 1951. I discuss Minoan and Greek use of landscape forms in detail in a forthcoming work, *The Earth, The Temple, and the Gods*.

40. Later gathered together: Sir Arthur J. Evans, *The Palace of Minos at Knossos*, 4 vols. and index in 7, London, 1921–1936.

41. *Ibid.*, vol. I, pp. 159–160. See also *idem*, "Mycenaean Tree and Pillar Cult," *Journal of Hellenic Studies*, 21, 1901, fig. 40, pp. 135ff, and *passim*.

42. As in the megalithic Maltese shrines. Cf. Sir T. Zammit, *Prehistoric Malta*, London, 1930. For a more general discussion of the whole tradition, see G. F. von Kaschnitz-Weinberg, *Die Mittelmeerischen Grundlagen der Antiken Kunst*, Frankfort, 1944.

43. *An American Architecture, op. cit.*, pp. 80–81.

44. Le Corbusier also studied Hadrian's villa and its Mediterranean prototypes, although he is concerned, as Wright was not, with an exterior expression, Hellenic in derivation, of the building as something other than a hollow: Cf. *Oeuvre Complète 1946–52*, 2nd enlarged edition, Zurich, 1955, pp. 24–31, 199–208. Also *Oeuvre Complète 1952–57*, Zurich, 1957, pp. 16–43, 56–65, 206–219. For further discussion of the differences between Wright and Le Corbusier and of the problem of "humanism" in architecture, see my article, cited Note 27, above.

45. *Architectural Forum*, June, 1959, p. 123.

46. *Op. cit.*, p. 138, fig. 21.

BIBLIOGRAPHICAL NOTE

A WORK OF this scale should stimulate further interest in its subject, but the bibliography on Wright is enormous and can hardly be listed here. Some of the major works have been mentioned in the notes. Wright's own literary production, beginning in 1894, was considerable, and it went on uninterruptedly until his death. It is listed, to 1940, in Frederick Gutheim's edition (*Frank Lloyd Wright On Architecture,* New York, 1941). The later titles are in Manson (*Frank Lloyd Wright to 1910,* New York, 1959). Wright's best and most illuminating writing is probably to be found in the *Autobiography* (1932, 1943), in the Princeton Lectures of 1930 (*Modern Architecture,* Princeton, 1931), and in the London Lectures of 1939 (*An Organic Architecture: The Architecture of Democracy,* London, 1939). Ideas embodied in some older, important articles—such as "The Art and Craft of the Machine," of 1901, and the series of nine, "In the Cause of Architecture," *Architectural Record,* 1928—are largely clarified and synthesized in those books. In *Genius and the Mobocracy,* New York, 1949, Wright gives a not very satisfactory account of his relationship with Sullivan. Later works, such as *The Future of Architecture,* New York, 1953, and *A Testament,* New York, 1957, tend to be repetitious of earlier statements. This is perfectly understandable in view of the attempt Wright was clearly making, both by building and writing, to round out his position in history before the end.

Hitchcock's *In the Nature of Materials, The Buildings of Frank Lloyd Wright, 1887–1941,* New York, 1942, remains the indispensable handbook for any study of Wright's architecture. It has a sound, informative text, 413 illustrations, and a chronological list of work. It should now be completed to 1959. Further illustrations of early work can be found in Manson (*op. cit.*) and in the contemporary architectural periodicals. References to these can be found in Gutheim and Manson. The German, Wasmuth volumes of 1910 and 1911, treated in the notes, are an excellent source of early drawings and photographs. The Dutch *Wendingen* publication of 1925 has some of the early buildings and work of the 'teens and early twenties as well. It includes articles by Wright, a touching tribute by Sullivan (who had been estranged from Wright for many years), and appreciations by a number of important European architects (usually listed:

Henricus T. Wijdeveld, ed., *The Life Work of the American Architect, Frank Lloyd Wright,* Santpoort, Holland, 1925). Wright drawings in color are reproduced in Heinrich de Fries, ed., *Frank Lloyd Wright; Aus dem Lebenswerke eines Architekten,* Berlin, 1926.

The splendid January, 1938, number of the *Architectural Forum* publishes the work of the thirties, as does the January, 1948, issue that of the forties. The work of Wright's last decade has been published only in scattered form. Some can be found in *Architectural Forum,* June, 1959, which briefly reviews Wright's whole career, some in *Architectural Record,* May, 1958, some in foreign periodicals such as *Casabella,* 227, May, 1959. The International exhibition of Wright's work, organized by Oskar Stonorov in 1951, had an excellent Swiss publication with some drawings in color (*Frank Lloyd Wright, Sechzig Jahre Lebendige Architektur,* Zurich, 1952). Many late as well as early drawings (plans, sections, elevations, and perspectives) are reproduced by Kaufmann (*An American Architecture,* New York, 1955; and *Taliesin Drawings, Recent Architecture of Frank Lloyd Wright,* New York, 1952).

Toward the end of his life, as at its first maturity (*Ladies Home Journal,* 1901, 1907), Wright's work had considerable popular publication (*House Beautiful,* 1955). More will undoubtedly come, because he was a synthesizer of traditions that go deep. Some of his late designs have been completed posthumously by the Taliesin Fellowship, and he has many followers (*House Beautiful,* 1959). It remains difficult for many of us to grasp the fact that there will be no new work of his own to see.

SELECTED CHRONOLOGICAL LIST OF
BUILDINGS AND PROJECTS (1889–1959)

1889	F. L. Wright House, Oak Park, Illinois.
1891	Charnley House, Chicago, Illinois.
1893	Winslow House, River Forest, Illinois.
1896	"Romeo and Juliet" Windmill, Spring Green, Wisconsin.
1898–1901	Golf Club, River Forest, Illinois.
1899	Husser House, Chicago, Illinois.
1900(?)–02	Ward Willitts House, Highland Park, Illinois.
1902	Heurtley House, Chicago, Illinois.
1902	Yahara Boat Club, Madison, Wisconsin. (Project)
1904	Martin House, Buffalo, New York.
1904	Larkin Building, Buffalo, New York. (Destroyed 1950)
1906	Unity Church, Oak Park, Illinois.
1906	Walter Gerts House, Glencoe, Illinois. (Project)
1908	Coonley House, Riverside, Illinois.
1908	Roberts House, River Forest, Illinois.
1909	Gale House, Oak Park, Illinois.
1909	Robie House, Chicago, Illinois.
1911	Taliesin East I, Spring Green, Wisconsin.
1912	Coonley Playhouse, Riverside, Illinois.
1914	Midway Gardens, Chicago, Illinois. (Destroyed 1923)
1915	A. D. German Warehouse, Richland Center, Wisconsin.
1916–1922	Imperial Hotel, Tokyo.
1920	Barnsdall House, Hollywood, California.
1922	Lake Tahoe Summer Colony Cabin, Lake Tahoe, California. (Project)
1923	Millard House, Pasadena, California.
1924	Freeman House, Los Angeles, California.
1929	St. Mark's Tower, New York. (Project)
1931–1935	Broadacre City. (Project)
1932	House on the Mesa. (Project)

1936–1937   Kaufmann House, "Falling Water," Connellsville, Pennsylvania.
1936–1939, 1950   Johnson Wax Administration Building, Racine, Wisconsin.
1937   Hanna House, Palo Alto, California.
1938–1959   Taliesin West, Maricopa Mesa, near Phoenix, Arizona.
1938   Florida Southern College, Lakeland, Florida.
1938   Ralph Jester House, Palos Verdes, California. (Project)
1939   First Herbert Jacobs House, Madison, Wisconsin.
1939   Goetsch-Winkler House, Okemos, Michigan.
1940   Lloyd Lewis House, Libertyville, Illinois.
1940   Pauson House, Phoenix, Arizona.
1942   Vigo Sundt House, Madison, Wisconsin. (Project)
1946–1959   Guggenheim Museum Solomon R., New York.
1947   Unitarian Church, Madison, Wisconsin.
1948   Second Jacobs House, Madison, Wisconsin.
1948–1949   Morris Gift Shop, San Francisco, California.
1950   Johnson Wax Building, Laboratory Tower, Racine, Wisconsin.
1952   David Wright House, Phoenix, Arizona.
1957   Grand Opera and Civic Auditorium, Bagdad, Iraq. (Project)
1959   Beth Sholom Synagogue, Elkins Park, Pennsylvania.
1959   Civic Center for Marin County, California. (Project)

SOURCES OF ILLUSTRATIONS

Wayne Andrews: 3, 19, 41, 47, 61, 64

Architectural Forum: Jan., 1938, 68, 69, 76, 78, 80, 81, 99; Jan., 1948, 82, 86, 91, 103, 104, 111, 121; June, 1959, 116, 127; May, 1958, 124

Architectural Record, 1906: 105

Courtesy Baltimore Museum of Art, Cone Collection, Baltimore, Maryland: 42

Fritz Burger, *Die Villen des Andrea Palladio* (Leipzig, 1910): 22 (top and bottom)

Chicago Architectural Photographing Company, Chicago, Illinois: 9, 10, 49, 50

George Cserna, New York: 117, 118, 119

Heinrich De Fries, ed., *Frank Lloyd Wright: Aus dem Lebenswerke eines Architekten* (Berlin, 1926): 36, 67

Paul Eluard, *Voir* (Geneva-Paris, 1948): 43

Sir Arthur J. Evans, *The Palace of Minos at Knossos* (London, 1921–36): 102; *The Mycenean Tree and Pillar Cult* (New York, 1901): 126

Reimar F. Frank, Milwaukee, Wisconsin: 100, 101

E. C. Gardner, *Illustrated Homes* (Boston, Massachusetts, 1875): 2

Laura Gilpin, Santa Fe, New Mexico: 60

P. E. Guerrero, New York: frontispiece, 77, 79, 89, 90, 92, 93, 94, 96, 113, 122, 123

Bill Hedrich, Hedrich-Blessing, Chicago, Illinois: 39, 72, 74, 75, 87, 88

Jeanneret-Gris, *Towards a New Architecture* (New York, 1929): 65

H. Kähler, *Hadrian und sein Villa bei Tivoli* (Berlin, 1959): 109

Torkel Korling, Dundee, Illinois: 98

Leavenworth's, Lansing, Michigan: 83, 85

Lou Lionni, New York: 120

Grant Manson, *Frank Lloyd Wright to 1910* (New York, 1958): 1, 11, 13, 16, 21, 24, 26

W. Albert Martin, Pasadena, California: 66

Collection Müller-Widmann, from Michel Seuphor, *Mondrian* (Basle, Switzerland): 55

Courtesy Museum of Modern Art, New York: 9, 16, 26, 45, 46, 49, 50, 56, 58, 68, 70, 71, 73, 74, 75, 77, 78, 83, 89, 90, 91, 100, 103, 104

Courtesy Richard J. Neutra, Los Angeles, California; Luckhaus Studio: 73

H. T. Palmer, San Francisco, California: 53

Maynard Parker, Los Angeles, California: 114, 115

Royal Institute of British Architects' Journal, vol. 27, 1920: 22 (center)

Courtesy Vincent J. Scully, Jr., New Haven, Connecticut: 97

G. W. Sheldon, *Artistic Country Seats* (New York, 1886–87): 4, 5

Courtesy Charles G. Solin, New Haven, Connecticut: 125

Ezra Stoller, Rye, New York: 44, 95, 106, 110, 112

Courtesy Verlag Wasmuth, *Ausgeführte Bauten und Entwürfe von Frank Lloyd Wright* (Berlin, 1910): 17, 18, 20, 25, 27, 29, 30, 31, 32, 34, 38, 40, 57; C. R. Ashbee, *Frank Lloyd Wright: Ausgeführte Bauten* (Berlin, 1911): 28, 33, 35, 37, 39, 54

Wendigen, 1929: 59, 63

Courtesy Frank Lloyd Wright Foundation and Henry-Russell Hitchcock, Jr., from *In the Nature of Materials: The Buildings of Frank Lloyd Wright* (New York, 1942): 6, 7, 12, 14, 15, 17, 23, 48, 51, 52, 71, 83, 84, 107

Courtesy Yale University Art Library, New Haven, Connecticut: 8, 62

T. Zammit, *The Neolithic Temples of Hal-Tarxien Malta* (Malta, 1927): 108

INDEX

The numerals in *italics* refer to the illustrations.